CONVERSATIONAL SPANISH:

QUICK AND EASY

BARBARA B. SALOOM
Endicott College

Copyright by Barbara B. Saloom
Fifth printing: 1993
ISBN: 0-9627755-0-9

Published by Professor Barbara B. Saloom, Boxford, Massachusetts
Telephone: 508-887-2581

To the many, many students who have helped me for fifteen years with their interest, enthusiasm and questions as we worked together to learn to "get along" in Spanish.

PREFACE

Many conversational Spanish books are available to students, but most of them presuppose some knowledge of Spanish, some experience with another foreign language, or an adequate knowledge of grammar. Many of the books are addressed to secondary school students and the material is not pertinent to an adult. Some beginners are frightened and give up because the material seems too difficult and/or the subject matter inadequate.

Conversational Spanish: Quick and Easy is presented to the adult or the college student who wants to attain a speaking knowledge of Spanish with the stress more on communication and comprehension than on grammatical depth. It is useful to tourists, business people who travel to Hispanic countries, people who deal with Hispanic people in the United States in the fields of medicine, dentistry, social work, small shops, etc. and those who want the enrichment and enjoyment of learning a foreign language.

This book accompanies a course that will be very useful to the student and still not intimidate or embarrass him with long grammatical terms; ie., demonstrative adjectives are called "Ways to say 'this' or 'that';" possessive adjectives are called "Ways to explain possession;" conjugations are explained in terms of how we explain who is performing the action; etc. Every student speaks many times during each lesson, and mistakes in grammar are minimized if not entirely overlooked. Again, the main purpose of the book is for the student to speak and to understand the spoken word, even if imperfectly. He is encouraged to use motions or descriptions in vocabulary with which he is acquainted if he does not know the exact vocabulary; ie., "facial tissues" could be "papel para la nariz" (paper for one's nose) or even "el Kleenex."

The general format of each lesson includes:
1. Vocabulary to be repeated many times in class and memorized, partially by classroom repetition but also at home, aloud, if possible.
2. Explanation: an informal explanation, in layman's terms, of grammar.
3. Culture: some description of Hispanic customs so that the American will not make an inappropriate remark to a Spanish- speaking person.
4. Practice: suggestions for impromptu dialogues and conversation. Grammatical exercises or explicit duplication of Spanish for English is

iii

purposely avoided so that the student can "think in Spanish" as much as possible in this short a course.

5. Extra vocabulary: Since a minium of vocabulary which the student can use to make himself understood is offered in the first part of each lesson, extra vocabulary is presented at its end for enrichment.

With the use of this book, students will be speaking Spanish to one another and to the teacher from the very first day of class. Emphasis is on repetition. Only the present tense is used in the first ten lessons. The future and a past tense are introduced in Lessons 11 through 15.

The lessons are kept light and personal so that the student is relaxed and, hopefully, even entertained. Use of the first name is encouraged, regardless of age.

There are two forms for "you" in Spanish, one used with close friends and relatives and one used with strangers or people in high positions. Since the student will probably be dealing with Hispanic people whom he does not know, the first ten chapters will use the formal "usted," and the informal "tú" will be introduced in Chapter 11.

Most Spanish speaking people talk a very similar language to the official language of Spain, Castilian. The main differences are the pronunciation of the "z," "c,"and "ll" and the use of the plural familiar form of "you." This book will use the Hispanic American "s" sound for both "z" and "c" rather than the "th" sound of Castilian, the "y" sound of "ll" instead of the "ly" Castilian sound and the "ustedes" form for the plural familiar "you" instead of the Castilian "vosotros." This usage will be understood throughout Spanish America and also in Spain.

Dear Teacher,

This type of course is a joy to teach. You have the ideal situation: your students <u>want</u> to learn Spanish. Undoubtedly, you have many ideas for the enrichment of the lessons. One that I have found to be meaningful to the adult student is the presentation of Spanish and Spanish American current events. Students often like to participate by bringing in their own travel or current event articles or telling about something they have seen or heard on television or radio. Many like to share with the class their experiences with Hispanics with whom they may work or whom they may have met abroad.

Any cultural material, such as, music or souvenirs of Spanish speaking countries, brought to class by the teacher or students, adds color and interest to the course. A Spanish American guest speaker, who talks to the class about his country, can expect many diverse questions from adult students.

Try to keep the conversation going in class by coming prepared with a long list of questions. Students seem to enjoy current, local, personal, and silly questions, such as, "¿Cómo se llama el presidente de los Estados Unidos?", "¿Qué hay en su refrigerador?", "¿Cuántas bocas tiene Luisa?"

An idea for a fun-type, as well as learning, experience is to form groups during class time, give each group a different, specific situation, and have them prepare their own dialogues. For example, "Mother, father, and their child (may be from three to 30 years old!) are discussing plans for the day. They cannot seem to come to an agreement and finally look at the clock and decide that it is too late to do anything."

Enjoy your students and your course!

Dear Student,

You may have learned a language taught in a more traditional way. The approach taken in this book will be different, but it will enable you to learn Spanish faster.

Most of the tools of the language are presented here, but some are not absolutely essential for your purpose, namely, "getting along in Spanish." Such things as accent marks and punctuation, use or omission of the subject pronouns, use of the personal "a" appear in the "Explanation" section, but you will be understood even if you do not remember all of the grammatical points.

Some advice which may help you is to memorize diligently the "Vocabulary" section. Practicing aloud is more effective for the student whose aim is primarily to speak and understand the language. Some students find it helpful to bring a tape recorder to class, some make flash cards and carry them about with them to use in spare moments, some listen to Spanish language programs on television or radio. Perhaps you can use your Spanish with a Spanish speaking person. Do whatever your situation permits to expose yourself as frequently as possible to the Spanish language.

¡Buena suerte!

CONTENTS

       Vocabulary Greetings, introductions, telling one's name, farewells
       Explanation Punctuation, abbreviations, conjugation
                       Verb   estar
       Culture   Hispanic names

       Vocabulary Useful expressions, nationalities, adjectives
       Explanation Small and capital letters, negative, questions, "ser" and "estar," gender, number
                       Verb   ser
       Culture   North Americans, South Americans, and Central Americans

       Vocabulary Family members, numbers, "ar" verbs
       Explanation Definite article, "ar" verbs, accent mark over question words, personal "a"
                       Verb   tener
       Culture   Hispanic family life

       Vocabulary Telling time, time expressions, weather expressions, "er" verbs, "tener" expressions, numbers
       Explanation How to tell time, "er" verbs, English translations of the present tense
                       Verb   ir
       Culture   The 24 hour clock and Spanish American attitudes toward time

Many thanks go to Virginia Cogger for her very careful editing of all aspects of the whole manuscript and to Dr. José Ricardo-Gil for his helpful comments on the Spanish phraseology.

Bart Addante guided us through the process of printing the book. The illustrations and cover were done by Mark Mrvicin . Thanks go to both for their skill and patience.

And much appreciation is extended to my husband, Dr. Joseph Saloom, for helping me with the complexities of the computer.

SPANISH PRONUNCIATION

Many people think that Spanish is the easiest language to learn. Perhaps they have this opinion because Spanish is a phonetic language and because there are definite rules that govern what syllables are to be stressed. Below you will find the Spanish alphabet and a guide to the pronunciation of each letter. It is not necessary to know the meaning of the word example. Just pronounce the word and get a feeling for the sound of the language.

a - a   cama, casa   Like English "ah," but shortened

b - be   banana, la Habana, ambos
     "B" and "v" are pronounced alike.
     When this letter appears at the beginning of a word group or before "m" or "n," it is pronounced like English "b." An example of the sound after "n" is given with the letter "v" since "n" rarely occurs before "b." When it appears between two vowels (a, e, i, o, u, y), it has a slightly different pronunciation. Prepare your lips as if you were going to pronounce the "b" sound but keep the center part of your lips open. If you have difficulty with this sound, don't worry about it. Many Spanish Americans use the English "v" sound.

c - ce   cena, cine
     cama, cosa, Cuba, secreto, clase
     Like English "s" before "e" and "i," like English "k" before "a," "o," and "u" or another consonant

ch - che muchacho, Chile
     "Ch" is considered one letter of the alphabet and is listed separately in the dictionary after the words that begin with "c." It is pronounced like the English "ch" in "chicken."

1

d - de   dama, cada
The "d" sound is softer than that of the English "d." The
tongue is placed against the inside of the upper front
teeth and the upper and lower teeth do not touch.
When "d" occurs between two vowels, it is even softer,
much like the "th" in "these."

e - e   mesa, cena
Pronounce the word "may." Notice that you are saying
two sounds. "May" has an "ee" sound after the "a."
Eliminate this last "ee" sound and you will be
pronouncing the Spanish "e".

f - efe   fama, gafas   Like English

g - ge   gemela, gitana
gala, gota, laguna
Like "c," "g" has two sounds. It is pronounced like English
"h" before "e" or "i" and like the hard "g" in "go" before
"a," "o," and "u."

h - hache   Habana, hada   Not pronounced

i - i   cine, gitano   Like English "ee" in "seen"

j - jota   jefe, paja   Like English "h"

l - ele   lana, alcalde   Like English, a little more lilting

ll - elle   calle, llama   Like English "y" in "yet." This is
also a separate letter of
the alphabet.

m - eme   medicina, mi   Like English

n - ene   lana, nada   Like English

ñ - eñe   mañana, señor
Another separate letter of the alphabet. It is pronounced like English "ny" in "canyon." The mark over the "n" is called a tilde.

o - o   mono, mano
Pronounce the word "go." Notice that you are saying two sounds. "Go" has an "oo" sound after the "o." Eliminate this last "oo" sound and you will be pronouncing the Spanish "o."

p - pe   para, depende   Like English

q - cu   que, aquello
As in English, "q" is followed by "u." The pronunciation of "qu" is that of English "k."

r - ere   madre, pero, alrededor, Enrique
This is probably the sound most different from English that we will learn. It is produced by vibrating the tongue against the tooth edge of the upper palate. The "tt" sound in the slang expression "Atta boy!" closely approximates the Spanish "r." It has the stronger sound of the next letter of the alphabet after the letters "l" and "n" and when it appears at the beginning of a word group.

rr - erre   perro, correr, ramo
Again we have a letter in the Spanish alphabet that we do not have in the English alphabet. It is pronounced like Spanish "r" but is trilled longer. There is also a slightly breathy sound that accompanies the trill.

s - ese   saber, Isabel
Usually pronounced like the soft "s" in the English word "some."

t - te   tema, Evita
"T," like "d," is softer than that of the English "t." The
teeth do not meet as they do to pronounce the English "t"
but rather the tongue is placed against the inside of the
upper front teeth.

u - u   una, puro
Like English sound of "oo" in "soon"

v - ve   vamos, ave, enviar
See "b" for pronunciation

x - equis expresar, exacto
Pronounced like an English soft "s"
before a consonant and like a "ks" as in
"excel" before a vowel

y - i griega ya, hoy   Pronounced like the Spanish "i"

z - zeta   zapatos, hazaña   Like English "s"

Often two or three vowels follow one another. Pronounce each vowel
and slide them together. The combinations will be with an "i," "y," or
"u":
baile, causa, agua, piano, hoy, Paraguay, buey

If there is no "i," "y," or "u," pronounce the two vowels as separate
syllables:
leo (le/o), creer (cre/er), aeroplano (a/eroplano)

Stress the next to the last syllable if the word ends in a vowel, "n" or
"s":
ensalada, muchacho, imposible, hablan, paraguas
For all other letters of the alphabet, stress the last syllable:
hotel, cantar, ciudad

Any syllable with a written accent receives the stress:
plátanos, está, días

LESSON 1

PRESENTACION

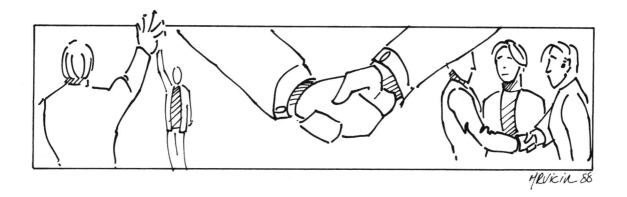

Buenos días, María.	Good day, good morning, Mary.
Buenas tardes, señor Alvarez.	Good afternoon, Mr. Alvarez.
Buenas noches, querido.	Good evening, good night, dear.
Hola, amigo.	Hello, buddy.

¿Cómo está usted, señor?	How are you sir?
Estoy muy bien, gracias.	I am very well, thank you, and
¿Y usted?	you?
Estoy mal hoy.	I am feeling bad today.
¿Cómo está Juan?	How is John?
Está bien, gracias.	He is well, thank you.
¿Cómo están Pedro y Ana?	How are Peter and Anna?
¿Cómo están ustedes?	How are you (plural)?
Estamos bien también.	We are also well.
Señor Johnson, quiero presentarle	Mr. Johnson, I'd like to introduce
al señor García.	Mr. Garcia to you.
Mucho gusto, señor García.	Pleased to meet you, Mr. García.
Igualmente.	The same to you.

(Notice that this last exchange would be "How do you do?" in English.)

¿Cómo se llama usted, señor?	What is your name, sir?
Me llamo Miguel López.	My name is Michael Lopez.
Y usted, señorita, ¿cómo se llama?	And you, Miss, what is your name?
Me llamo Alicia González.	My name is Alice Gonzalez.

5

¿Cómo se llama la señora?	What is the lady's name?
Se llama Ana Navarro de López.	Her name is Anna Navarro López.
¿Cómo se llaman los niños?	What are the children's names?
Se llaman Paco, Adela, y Carmen.	Their names are Frank, Adele, and Carmen.

Adiós, Pablo.	Good-bye, Paul.
Hasta luego, Ana.	So long, Anna.
Hasta la vista, Ana.	So long, Anna.
Hasta mañana, Juan.	See you tomorrow, John.

EXPLANATION:

1. In reading Spanish, one can tell immediately from the punctuation whether a statement, question, or exclamation is to follow. Notice the inverted question marks introducing the questions in the above vocabulary. Examples of exclamations are:

¡Ay, Dios mío!	Oh, my goodness!
¡Caramba!	Good gracious!

2. Abbreviations:

señor	Sr.
señora	Sra.
señorita	Srta.
usted	Ud.
ustedes	Uds.

The abbreviation is capitalized.
Use the word "the" with the titles "Sr., " Sra.," and "Srta.," when talking about someone.

El Sr. García está bien.
La Srta. Alicia González no está bien.

The word "the" is not necessary in direct address.

¿Cómo está Ud., Sr,?

3.

estar - to be

yo estoy	I am	nosotros (as) estamos	we are
él está	he is	ellos están	they are
ella está	she is	ellas están	they (fem.)are
usted está	you are	ustedes están	you (pl) are

Each subject pronoun (I, he, she, you (singular), we, they, you (plural)) has a certain form of the verb "to be" which must be used with it. Just as we would not say in English "I is," we would not say in Spanish "yo está" but rather, "yo estoy," if we meant "I am." These forms must be memorized as we learn new verbs. They come naturally to the native speaker, but, since we are not native Latins, we resort to a function called "conjugation" to help us learn the verbs. You have seen above the partial conjugation of the verb "to be" or "estar." The conjugation is partial because it does not include the two forms used for "you" (tú and vosotros). These are used in addressing very close friends, relatives, servants, and pets and will be discussed later in the text. The "we" form has two different endings: "nosotros" refers to males or to a group of male(s) and female(s) and "nosotras" refers only to females. "Ellos," "they" refers to a group of males or to a group of male(s) and female(s), and "ellas," "they" refers only to females. "Usted," "you" is used when talking to one person: "ustedes" to more than one.

In the vocabulary listing, we did not say "Yo estoy muy bien, gracias" but simply "Estoy muy bien, gracias." Unless there is confusion as to who is involved, Spanish-speaking people do not use the subject pronouns except "usted" and "ustedes." These are used as a form of courtesy to the person being addressed.

CULTURE:

Spanish speaking people use the name of the person being addressed whenever possible (Buenas tardes, Sr. Alvarez.). If they do not know the name, they use "señor," "señora," or "señorita" (¿Cómo está Ud., Sr.?). They usually shake hands when meeting. If they are friends, women kiss each other on each cheek and hold hands; men hug each other and sometimes pat each other's back while hugging. In an Hispanic country we should offer our hand when being introduced.

Names are a little different among Hispanics. Ana Navarro de López' maiden name is Navarro and she married someone named López. She keeps her maiden name and attaches her husband's name. The "de," "of" is short for "esposa de," "wife of." Today we might also say Ana Navarro-López or Ana Navarro López.

Some Spanish names taken from the Catholic religion (Jesús or Concepción) may not sound familiar to us. Some men may have the name María.

7

PRACTICE:
USE A COMPLETE SENTENCE IN ALL THE PRACTICE DRILLS
THROUGHOUT THE BOOK.

1. Each student turns to the student to his right and asks him in
Spanish what his name is. The second student tells him his name,
and this exercise is continued until everyone has spoken
individually.

2. Each student turns to the student to his right and introduces to
him the student to his left. Both students acknowledge the
introduction. Keep this practice up until every student has
participated.

3. Students greet one another by name and ask each other how they
are or how someone else is. Try to vary the exchange by addressing
two people or asking someone the name of others in the class.

EXTRA VOCABULARY:
¡ajá! aha!
así, así so, so (all right)
Bienvenido! Welcome!
¡Chao! Bye!
chica, la young girl
chico, el young boy, guy
El gusto es mío. My pleasure.(response to an introduction)
Encantado. Delighted.
mejor better
placer, el pleasure
¿Qué tal? How's it going?
Saludos a María. Greetings or regards to Mary.

LESSON 2

VAMOS A HABLAR

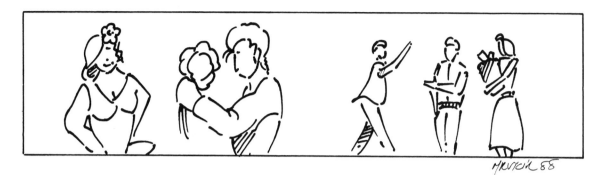

Sí	Yes
No	No
Por favor	Please
Muchas gracias	Thank you very much
De nada	You're welcome
No hay de qué	You're welcome.
Perdón	Forgive me (for something I've done)
Con permiso	Excuse me, with your permission (for something I'm about to do: ie. pass in front of someone, leave the room, eat in someone's presence)
No sé.	I don't know.
No entiendo.	I don't understand.
Repita Ud., por favor.	Please repeat.
Hablo poco español.	I speak very little Spanish.
Más despacio, por favor.	More slowly, please.
¿Cómo se dice en español_____?	How does one say_____ in Spanish?
¿Es Ud. puertorriqueño?	Are you Puerto Rican?
No, soy norteamericano.	No, I am American.
¿Son ustedes puertorriqueños?	Are you Puerto Rican?
No, somos argentinos.	No, we are Argentinian.
Es Clara norteamericana?	Is Clara American?
No, no es norteamericana.	No, she is not American.

¿Son mexicanos Alberto y Juan?	Are Albert and John Mexican?		
¿Son argentinas Isabel y María?	Are Elizabeth and Mary Argentinians?		
No, Isabel y María no son argentinas.	No, Elizabeth and Mary are not Argentinians.		

bueno	good	grande	big
malo	bad	pequeño	small
mucho	a lot of, much	contento	happy
poco	a little, few	triste	sad
rico	rich	enfermo	sick
pobre	poor	cansado	tired
fácil	easy	simpático	nice
difícil	difficult		

EXPLANATION:
1. Nationalities are written with a small letter:
   ¿Es usted mexicano?
   No, soy norteamericano.

2. To make a word plural in Spanish, add "s" to words that end in a vowel and "es" to words that end in a consonant:

argentino	Argentinian	argentinos	Argentinians
mexicano	Mexican	mexicanos	Mexicans
mujer	woman	mujeres	women
ciudad	city	ciudades	cities

3. To make a sentence negative, we put the word "no" before the verb:
   No es norteamericano.
   No, Isabel y María no son argentinas.

4. The most usual way to form a question is to invert the subject and verb:
   ¿Es usted mexicano?
   ¿Son ustedes puertorriqueños?

10

However, if the subject is longer than what follows the verb, we put it at the end:

¿Son mexicanos Alberto y Juan?

¿Son argentinas Isabel y María?

5.   ser - to be

(yo) soy	I am	(nosotros/as) somos	we are
(él) es	he is	(ellos) son	they are
(ella) es	she is	(ellas) son	they are
usted es	you are	ustedes son	you are

6. In Spanish there are two verbs meaning "to be." Each verb has different uses:

"Ser" is used if the noun (name of a person or thing) following it is the same person as the subject:

Somos argentinos.	We are Argentinians. ("We" and "Argentinians" are the same people.)
¿Son Uds. puerto-rriqueños?	Are you Puerto Ricans? ("You" and "Puerto Ricans" are the same people.)

It is also used with an adjective that describes a characteristic, usually permanent, of a person or thing:

El Sr. Menéndez es rico.	Mr. Menendez is rich.
El español es fácil.	Spanish is easy.

"Estar" is used to express location:

Miami está en Florida.	Miami is in Florida.
Estamos en clase.	We are in class.

It is also used with an adjective that describes a condition, usually temporary, of a person or thing:

Manuel está enfermo.	Manuel is sick.
María está cansada.	Mary is tired.

7. Gender plays a larger part in Spanish than it does in English. When we are describing a masculine person or thing, the ending of the adjective is often "o":

Manuel está enfermo.	Manuel is sick.
El Sr. Menéndez es rico.	Mr. Menendez is rich.

When we are describing a feminine person or thing, the ending of the adjective is often "a."

María está cansada.   Mary is tired.

¿Es Clara norteamericana?   Is Clara American?

Descriptive words which do not end in "o" (pobre, fácil, difícil, grande, triste) stay the same in the masculine and feminine:

Pedro es grande.	Peter is big.
Elena es grande también.	Helen is also big.

8. Number also has to be taken into consideration more often in Spanish than in English. If a noun being described is plural, we must add "s" to descriptive words that end in a vowel and "es" to words that end in a consonant.

Ellos son grandes.	They are big.
Nosotros estamos enfermos.	We are sick.
Las lecciones son difíciles.	The lessons are difficult.
Ellas están cansadas.	They are tired.

("Lecciones" is a feminine noun. We will discuss things, rather than persons, which are masculine and feminine in Lesson 4.)

CULTURE:

People from North America are "norteamericanos"; from Central America, "centroamericanos"; and from South America; "sudamericanos." Some Spanish Americans might resent our calling ourselves "americanos," since they are also "Americans." So that they will not think that we feel that we have a priority on being called "Americans," it is more tactful for us to say, "Soy norteamericano" even though Spanish Americans themselves refer to us as "americanos" and themselves as "latinos."

PRACTICE:

1. Quiz each other on the vocabulary learned up to now by asking, "¿Cómo se dice en español (English word or expression)?"

2. Ask each other questions using the vocabulary learned in Lessons 1 and 2.

3. Using the nationalities and descriptive words you have learned up to now, ask each other questions. Examples: ¿Es simpática María?, ¿Está usted enfermo?, ¿Son simpáticos Juan y Pablo?

EXTRA VOCABULARY:
A ver. Let's see.
adelante straight ahead
agradable pleasant
al contrario on the contrary
atrás backward, behind
¿Dígame? Pardon me? (I didn't hear you)
eficiente efficient
fantástico fantastic
favorito favorite
feo ugly
hermoso beautiful, lovely
importante important
joven young
loco crazy, mad
maravilloso marvelous
más que nunca more than ever
¡No me digas! You don't say!
nuevo new
popular popular
¿Qué hay de nuevo? What's new?
¿Quién sabe? Who knows?
un momento just a minute
viejo old

LESSON 3

LA FAMILIA

el padre	the father
la madre	the mother
los padres	the parents
el hijo	the son
la hija	the daughter
los hijos	the sons, the children
el hermano	the brother
la hermana	the sister
los hermanos	the brothers, the brothers and sisters
el abuelo	the grandfather
la abuela	the grandmother
los abuelos	the grandparents

¿Habla Ud. español?	Do you speak Spanish?
Sí, hablo español.	Yes, I speak Spanish.
Y mis padres también hablan español.	And my parents also speak Spanish.
Pero hablamos inglés en casa.	But we speak English at home.
Mi tío habla inglés con mi tía.	My uncle speaks English with my aunt
Mis tíos hablan poco español.	My aunt and uncle speak little Spanish.
hay	there is, there are
¿Hay muchos puertorriqueños en Nueva York?	Are there many Puerto Ricans in New York?
Sí, y hay muchos cubanos en Miami.	Yes, and there are many Cubans in Miami.
No hay muchos mexicanos en Maine.	There are not many Mexicans in Maine.

¿Cuántos hijos tiene Ud.?	How many children do you have?
Tengo tres hijos.	I have three children.
¿Dónde están los hijos?	Where are the children?
Visitan a los parientes.	They are visiting relatives.
¿Por qué están en California?	Why are they in California?
¿Cuándo llegan Uds. a México?	When are you arriving in México?
Llegamos mañana.	We are arriving tomorrow.
¿Cómo viaja Ud.?	How are you traveling?
Viajo en avión.	I am traveling by airplane.
¿Quién acompaña a los abuelos?	Who is accompanying the grandparents?
Nadie acompaña a los abuelos.	No one is accompanying the grandparents.
¿Qué desean los amigos?	What do the friends want?
Desean comer en seguida.	They want to eat immediately.

uno	one
dos	two
tres	three
cuatro	four
cinco	five
seis	six
siete	seven
ocho	eight
nueve	nine
diez	ten

EXPLANATION:

1. The word "the" has four forms in Spanish depending upon the gender and number of the noun they precede:

el hijo	the son (masculine, singular)
la hija	the daughter (feminine, singular)
los hombres	the men (masculine, plural)
las mujeres	the women (feminine, plural)

2.
hablar - to speak

Spanish	English	Spanish	English
(yo) hablo	I speak	(nosotros/as) hablamos	we speak
(él) habla	he speaks	(ellos) hablan	they speak
(ella) habla	she speaks	(ellas) hablan	they speak
Ud. habla	you speak	Uds. hablan	you speak

In order to conjugate (see Lesson 1, Explanation 3) a verb that ends in "ar," we remove the "ar" ending and are left with the stem, "habl." To this stem we add "o" to express "I speak," "a" to express "he," "she," or "you" (sing) speak, "amos" to mean "we" speak and "an" for "they" or "you" (pl) speak. Any regular verb, ending in "ar" may be treated in this same manner.

3. Verbs that have a pattern like the above for conjugating are called "regular" verbs. Spanish, like English, has irregular verbs as we have learned from our study of "estar" and "ser." These verbs must be memorized. Irregular verbs that are used frequently will be presented in the first ten lessons.

4.   tener - to have

(yo) tengo	I have	(nosotros/as)tenemos	we have
(él) tiene	he has	(ellos) tienen	they have
(ella) tiene	she has	(ellas) tienen	they have
Ud. tiene	you have	Uds. tienen	you have.

After this lesson, the Spanish verb forms will be presented without the subjects.

5. In addition to the inverted question mark, the question word which introduces the interrogative, bears an accent mark over the stressed vowel:

> ¿Cuántos hijos tiene Ud.?
> ¿Cómo viajan?

6. When the action of the verb is directly on a person, rather than a thing, we use "a" in front of the person. After "tener," "to have," we do not use this personal "a."

> Visitan a los parientes.
> ¿Quién acompaña a los abuelos?
> Tengo tres hijos.

CULTURE:
The Hispanic family, which often includes the extended family, is more closely knit than the American family. They almost always have their meals together and they linger over these meals and converse a great deal. The children usually live at home until they get married. The father is the head of the family and makes most of

the decisions, but the mother's influence is also very strong. The children's godparents are considered members of the extended family.

Today, with advanced communication, customs are changing, particularly in large cities, and we find the lifestyle of many Hispanics to be very similar to ours. In general, however, the Hispanic life is still more conservative than that of the United States.

PRACTICE:
1. Ask each other questions beginning with the question words; cuántos, cuántas, dónde, por qué, cuándo, cómo, quién, and qué.

2. Use the "ar" verbs presented in this lesson (llegar, viajar, acompañar, desear) with varied subjects. Examples: María desea hablar. Viajo a México. Llegamos a California. Paco y Julio acompañan a los abuelos.

3. Prepare two questions, using the material learned in this lesson, to ask your classmates.

4. Count from one to ten. Count from ten to one.

EXTRA VOCABULARY:
¡Basta! That will do!
compañero de cuarto, el roommate (m)
compañera de cuarto, la roommate (f)
cuñada, la sister-in-law
cuñado, el brother-in-law
enfadado angry
gato, el cat
gente, la people
hombre, el man
luna de miel, la honeymoon
matrimonio, el married couple
mimado spoiled
mujer, la woman
nieta, la grandaughter
nieto, el grandson
nuera, la daughter-in-law
orgulloso proud
pájaro, el bird

perro, el dog
persona, la person
prima, la cousin (f)
primo, el cousin (m)
sacar fotos to take snapshots
saludar to greet
sobrina, la niece
sobrino, el nephew
suegra, la mother-in-law
suegro, el father-in-law
tonto stupid, foolish
viuda, la widow
viudo, el widower
yerno, el son-in-law

LESSON 4

LA HORA Y EL TIEMPO

¿Qué hora es?	What time is it?
Es la una.	It is one o'clock.
Es la una y diez.	It's ten after one.
Son las cuatro.	It's four o'clock.
Son las siete y cinco.	It's five after seven.
Son las ocho menos veinte.	It's 20 of eight.
Son las dos y media.	It's half past two.
Es la una y cuarto.	It's quarter after one.
Son las tres menos cuarto.	It's quarter of three.
¿A qué hora llega Ud.?	At what time are you arriving?
a las nueve de la mañana	at nine in the morning (A.M.)
a las tres de la tarde	at three in the afternoon (P.M.)
a las ocho de la noche (P.M.)	at eight o' clock in the evening
Es mediodía.	It is noon.
Es medianoche.	It is midnight.

¿Adónde van las niñas?	Where are the little girls going?
Van a la escuela por la mañana.	They go to school in the morning.
Voy a casa por la tarde.	I go home in the afternoon.
Es temprano.	It is early.
Ya es tarde.	It is late.
¿Qué tiempo hace hoy?	What is the weather like today?
Hace buen tiempo.	It is nice weather.
Hace mal tiempo.	It is bad weather.
Hace viento.	It is windy.

Hace (mucho) frío.	It is (very) cold.
Hace (mucho) calor.	It is (very) hot.
Hace fresco.	It is cool.
Hace (or "hay") sol.	It is sunny.
Está lloviendo.	It is raining.
Llueve.	It is raining.
Está nevando.	It is snowing.
Nieva.	It is snowing.
Comemos cada día.	We eat every day.
Corro a la playa.	I am running to the beach.
Mario debe llevar el paraguas.	Mario ought to take the umbrella.
Los niños aprenden a nadar.	The children are learning to swim.
Gloria comprende la lección.	Gloria understands the lesson.
Juan lee el periódico.	John is reading the newspaper.
Juanita vende refrescos.	Juanita sells cold drinks.
Bebemos cerveza.	We drink beer.
Tengo hambre.	I am hungry.
Ud. tiene razón.	You are right.
Tenemos miedo.	We are afraid.
Los niños tienen sueño.	The children are sleepy.
Paco tiene sed.	Frank is thirsty.
Hoy tenemos calor.	Today we are warm.
Uds. tienen frío.	You are cold.
¿Cuántos años tiene Ud.?	How old are you?
Tengo veinte años.	I am twenty years old.

once	eleven	dieciséis	sixteen
doce	twelve	diecisiete	seventeen
trece	thirteen	dieciocho	eighteen
catorce	fourteen	diecinueve	nineteen
quince	fifteen	veinte	twenty

EXPLANATION:
1. To tell time, use the expression, "Es" and the number one "la una" for "It is one o'clock" but "Son" with "las" and the appropriate number for "It is two o'clock" and later.

> Es la una
> Son las cuatro.

22

To tell how many minutes after the hour it is, add the word "y," (and) and the number of minutes. To tell how many minutes before the hour it is, add the word "menos," (less) and the number of minutes. "Half past" is "media," and "a quarter of an hour" is "cuarto."

Son las siete y cinco.
Son las ocho menos veinte.
Son las dos y media.
Es la una y cuarto.

2.   comer - to eat

como	I eat	comemos	we eat
come	he, she eats	comen	they, you eat
	you eat		

In order to conjugate a verb that ends in "er," remove the "er" ending and to the stem, "com," add "o" to express "I eat," "e" to express "he," "she," or "you" (sing) eat, "emos" to mean "we eat," and "en" for "they" and "you" (pl) eat.

After this lesson, the English meanings will be given only for the infinitive form. Infinitives, which are expressed in English with the word "to" and the verb (to speak, to eat, to live), have an ending of "ar," "er," or "ir" in Spanish (hablar, comer, vivir).

3. Every Spanish noun has gender. Nouns that end in "o" are almost always masculine and nouns that end in "a" are almost always feminine (el periódico and la cerveza). Memorize nouns along with the Spanish word for "the" (el paraguas, la tarde).

4.   ir - to go

voy	I go	vamos	we go
va	he, she goes	van	they, you go
	you go		

The word "a" follows the verb "to go."

Voy a la playa.   I am going to the beach.

Va a llegar a las dos.   He (she) is going to arrive at two o'clock.

5. This book deals mostly with present time. The Spanish form for a present tense verb has three English translations:

Voy.	I go, am going, do go.
Viajamos.	We travel, are traveling, do travel.
¿Habla Ud. español?	Do you speak Spanish? ¿Are you speaking Spanish?
Bebemos cerveza.	We drink beer. We are drinking beer. We do drink beer.

CULTURE:

To express scheduled events (theater, trains, airplanes, etc.), Spanish American countries use the twenty-four hour system. One o'clock in the morning follows midnight and is "la una." One o'clock in the afternoon is "las trece," two o'clock, "las catorce," three o'clock, "las quince," etc.

In general, Spanish Americans are not as prompt as North Americans. It is helpful to know that these cultural differences exist in order to prevent misunderstandings. We must not become angry if an Hispanic is late for an appointment and they should not think of us as "uptight " because we arrive on time.

PRACTICE:

1. ¿Qué hora es?   Answer in a complete Spanish sentence.

a. 3:08 P.M.   f. quarter of two
b. 10:15 A.M.   g. midnight
c. 5:30   h. 4:15
d. 20 of six   i. noon
e. 1:18   j. five of seven

2. A student calls upon another and asks, "¿Qué tiempo hace?". The student called upon answers with any weather expression, then calls upon another student who uses a different response. This continues until each student has responded.

3. Ask questions of other students using a verb from the conjugation that ends in "er" (comer, aprender, comprender, correr, leer, vender, deber, beber). Examples: ¿Cuántos niños aprenden español? ¿Qué lee el niño? ¿Vende Ud. cerveza? ¿Comen Uds. a las siete?

4. Ask questions of other students using the "tener" expressions. Examples: ¿Quién tiene sueño?   ¿Tiene Ud. razón?   ¿Cuántos años tiene el señor?

5. Go around the class giving each other mathematical problems: Examples:

¿Cuántos son tres y cinco?	How much are three and five?
Tres y cinco son ocho.	Three and five are eight.
¿Cuántos son diecinueve menos cuatro?	How much are nineteen minus four?
Diecinueve menos cuatro son quince.	Nineteen minus four are fifteen.

6. You now know how to greet each other, make introductions, take leave of one another, tell nationalities, discuss your family, describe people, tell what time it is and at what time you do a certain activity, what the weather is like, people's ages, etc. Form into groups of two or three, take ten or fifteen minutes to prepare a conversation, and then present your conversation to the class.

EXTRA VOCABULARY:
a la vez   at the same time
a menudo   often
ahora mismo   right now
al principio   at first
calendario, el   calendar
casi   almost
cielo, el   sky
clima, el   climate
día de fiesta, el   holiday
día de trabajo, el   work day
¡Eso es!   That's right!
estación, la   season
fecha, la   date
hielo, el   ice
hoy en día   nowadays
invierno, el   winter
lluvia, la   rain
más tarde   later
minuto, el   minute
mojado   wet
nieve, la   snow

otoño, el   autumn
poco a poco   little by little
primavera, la   spring
relámpago, el   lightning
seco   dry
segundo, el   second
siguiente   following
temprano   early
tener éxito   to be successful
todos los días   every day
tormenta, la   storm
trueno, el   thunder
verano, el   summer

LESSON 5

LOS OFICIOS

¿Qué trabajo hace Ud.?	What kind of work do you do?
Soy ingeniero.	I am an engineer.
Y Ud., ¿qué trabajo hace?	And what kind of work do you do?
Soy mecánico/a.	I am a mechanic.
Y mi primo/a es secretario/a.	And my cousin is a secretary.
Nuestros/as hermanos/as son enfermeros/as.	Our sisters/brothers are nurses.
Los médicos tienen que trabajar mucho.	Doctors have to work a lot.
Las amas de casa trabajan en casa.	Homemakers work at home.
Los estudiantes y los profesores trabajan en la escuela.	Students and teachers work at school.
Algunos abogados ganan mucho dinero.	Some lawyers earn a lot of money.
Su primo es un carpintero muy diligente.	His cousin is a very industrious carpenter.
El lunes, van a casa con el señor Franco.	On Monday they are going home with Mr. Franco
Los cocineros y los camareros tra_ bajan en un restaurante.	Cooks and waiters work in a restaurant.
Los barberos y los peluqueros tra_ bajan en una peluquería.	Barbers and hair dressers work in a barber shop (or hairdresser's).
Miguel quiere ser arquitecto.	Michael wants to be an architect.
El quiere mucho a Linda.	He loves Linda a lot.

27

a	to, at
en	in, on
de	of, from
con	with

¿Le gusta a Ud. jugar al tenis?	Do you like to play tennis?
Sí, me gusta.	Yes, I do.
Nos gusta jugar al béisbol.	We like to play baseball.
Les gusta ir al cine el sábado.	They like to go to the movies on Saturday.

Vivimos en los Estados Unidos.	We live in the United States.
Escribo una carta.	I am writing a letter.
Francisco recibe una tarjeta postal de su madre.	Francis receives a postcard from his mother.
Abren la puerta de la escuela.	They are opening the door of the school.

¿Qué día es hoy?	What day is today?
Hoy es:	Today is:

lunes	Monday	viernes	Friday
martes	Tuesday	sábado	Saturday
miércoles	Wednesday	domingo	Sunday
jueves	Thursday		

veintiuno	21	cuarenta y uno, etc.	41
veintidós	22	cincuenta	50
veintitrés	23	sesenta	60
veinticuatro,etc.	24	setenta	70
treinta	30	ochenta	80
treinta y uno	31	noventa	90
treinta y dos, etc.	32	ciento	100
cuarenta	40		

EXPLANATION:
1. The words for "a" or "an" in Spanish are "un" before a masculine word and "una" before a feminine word:

un restaurante
una peluquería

28

2. In telling one's occupation in Spanish, we do not use the word "a" (un, una) unless the occupation is modified (described):

> Soy ingeniero.
> Mi prima es secretaria.
> Su primo es un carpintero muy inteligente.

3. Possession:

The words that express possession agree with the thing that is possessed. If the thing possessed is plural, add "s" to the possessive. In the case of "nuestro" (our), change "o" to "a" if the thing possessed is feminine.

mi amigo	my friend
mis amigos	my friends
su amigo	his, her, their, your friend
sus amigos	his, her, their, your friends
nuestro amigo	our friend (m)
nuestra amiga	our friend (f)
nuestros amigos	our friends (all masc. or masc. and fem.)
nuestras amigas	our friends (f)

4. gustar - to be pleasing to (to like)

"Me gusta" means "I like"; "le gusta", "he", "she" or "you" like; "nos gusta", "we like"; and "les gusta", "they" or plural "you" like.

¿Le gusta a Ud. jugar al tenis?	Is playing tennis pleasing to you?
Sí, me gusta.	Yes, it is pleasing to me.
Nos gusta jugar al béisbol.	Playing baseball is pleasing to us.
Les gusta ir al cine.	Going to the movies is pleasing to them.

5. The days of the week are written with a small letter although one sees the capital letter used frequently nowadays. To say "on a given day," use "el" and the day of the week:

> Les gusta ir al cine el sábado.
> El lunes van a casa con el señor Franco.

6. Verbs that end in "ir" are conjugated in the same way as those that end in "er" except for the "we" form which ends in "imos":

vivir - to live

vivo	vivimos
vive	viven

7.

querer - to love, to want

quiero	queremos
quiere	quieren

8. Contrary to English usage, words used in a general sense, require the word "the" before them:

> Los médicos tienen que trabajar mucho.
> Las amas de casa trabajan en casa.

CULTURE:

The equal rights movement is going on in Spanish America and Spain just as it is in other countries, and so we have the emergence of new vocabulary such as, "la médica" for a woman doctor and "el enfermero" for a male nurse.

Many middle and upper class Hispanics feel that manual work is demeaning. College students prefer clerical work to waiting on tables, even though office work may pay less. The emphasis among Hispanic people is not on work and money but rather family and friends. Many are sentimental by our standards and, though prepared by their education to be doctors or lawyers, may also write poetry, novels, or essays.

The Spanish calendar shows Monday as the first day of the week and is sometimes confusing to the American, who is accustomed to seeing Sunday as the first day.

Soccer (called "fútbol" in Spanish) is the most popular sport in Spanish America. Baseball is also very popular, particularly in those countries closest to the United States (Mexico, Central America, and the Caribbean islands). Other favorites are basketball and tennis.

PRACTICE:

1. Tell what you plan to do each day. Examples: El lunes voy al restaurante. El martes voy a escribir muchas cartas., El miércoles tengo que trabajar., etc.

2. Each student recites one consecutive number from one to one hundred, in turn, first counting by one, then ten, then five, and then two.

3. Each student asks two questions of her classmates, one, using an expression with "gustar", and one with "querer". Examples: ¿Quiere Ud. viajar a México? ¿Les gusta leer el periódico?

4. Ask questions of other students using a verb from the conjugation that ends in "ir" (vivir, escribir, recibir, abrir). Examples: ¿Quién abre la puerta? ¿Qué reciben Uds.?

5. Form into groups of two or three and take ten or fifteen minutes to prepare a conversation about your work. Use your imagination. You might like or not like your work. Perhaps you work in a different country. Maybe you work with a relative or friend. See if your fellow students show by their reaction that they understand what you are saying by injecting some humor into your dialogue.

EXTRA VOCABULARY:
actor, el   actor
actriz, la   actress
artista, el, la   artist
astronauta, el, la   astronaut
cliente, el, la   client, customer
compañía, la   company
cura, el   priest
de vez en cuando   from time to time
dependiente/a el, la   clerk (in a store)
derecho, el   right
despedir (i)   to fire
detective privado, el   private detective
diplomática, la   diplomat
diplomático, el   diplomat
empleada, la   employee

31

empleado, el employee
empleo, el job
en vez de instead of
enseñar to teach
estudiar to study
famoso famous
fracaso, el failure
habilidad, la skill, ability
hay que one must
hombre de negocios, el business man
jefa, la boss, manager
jefe, el boss, manager
merecer to deserve
negocios, los business
oficina, la office
periodista, el, la journalist
premio, el prize
profesión, la profession
profesor, el professor
profesora, la professor
programador de computadoras, el computer programmer (m)
programadora de computadoras, la computer programmer (f)
psicólogo, el psychologist (m)
psicóloga, la psychologist (f)
soldado, el soldier
solicitar un empleo to apply for a job
sueldo, el salary
Yo no. Not me.

LESSON 6

LA CASA

MRVICIK 88

¿Dónde vive Ud?
Where do you live?

Vivo en una ciudad cerca de
Boston.
I live in a city near Boston.

Mi casa es grande: tiene muchos
cuartos.
My house is big: it has many
rooms.

Tiene sala, comedor, cocina, dos ba_
ños, y cuatro dormitorios.
It has a living room, dining
room, kitchen , two bathrooms,
and four bedrooms.

También tiene sótano y trascocina.
It also has a basement and a
utility room.

La casa de mi abuelo es pequeña.
My grandfather's house is small.

Tomamos el desayuno y el almuerzo
en la cocina y la cena en el comedor.
We have breakfast and lunch
in the kitchen, and supper in
the dining room.

A veces tomamos la merienda al
aire libre.
Sometimes we have our
afternoon snack outdoors.

Tenemos lavadora y refrigerador.
We have a washing machine
and a refrigerator.

A menudo tenemos visita.
We often have company.

Entonces jugamos al bridge-contrato
y tomamos un bocadillo y gaseosa
o vino.
Then we play bridge and we
have a bite to eat and soda
or wine.

Los niños juegan en el patio.
The children play in the yard.

Cuando no tenemos visita, leemos
revistas y libros, pagamos cuentas,
charlamos, trabajamos en el jardín,
o descansamos.
When we don't have
company, we read magazines
and books, we pay bills, we
chat, we work in the garden,
or we rest.

Cada semana limpiamos la casa.	Every week we clean the house.		

Nuestra casa está en la Calle Roble en el pueblo de San Luis.
Our house is on Roble Street `in the town of San Luis.

A la derecha hay una tienda de ropa.
There is a clothing store to the right.

A la izquierda hay una farmacia.
There is a drugstore to the left.

Es la farmacia del Sr. Sánchez.
It is Mr. Sanchez' drugstore.

Hay muchas carreteras en mi ciudad.
There are many highways in my city.

Hay edificios altos y casas pequeñas.
There are tall buildings and small houses.

Tenemos una universidad y varias iglesias y escuelas.
We have a university and several churches and schools.

Me gustan los edificios altos.
I like tall buildings.

Le gustan las casas pequeñas.
He (she, you) likes small houses.

enero	January	julio	July
febrero	February	agosto	August
marzo	March	septiembre	September
abril	April	octubre	October
mayo	May	noviembre	November
junio	June	diciembre	December

¿Cuál es la fecha de hoy?
What is today's date?

Hoy es el primero de septiembre.
Today is September 1.

Mañana es el tres de agosto.
Tomorrow is August 3.

Es el dieciocho de enero.
It is January 18.

EXPLANATION:

In Spanish, the word "the" is used with meals:

> Tomamos el desayuno y el almuerzo en la cocina y la cena en el comedor.

2. To express possession in Spanish, the word "de" is used between the thing possessed and the possessor:

> La casa de mi abuelo es pequeña.
> Es la familia del Sr. Sánchez.

3. Gustar - to be pleasing to, to like
When the thing liked is plural, use "gustan":

Me gustan los edificios altos.   Tall buildings are pleasing to
                                   me.

Le gustan las casas pequeñas.   Small houses are pleasing to
                                   him, her, you.

4. The words "a" and "el" are contracted to form "al." "De" and "el" are contracted to form "del":

        Jugamos al bridge-contrato.
        Es la farmacia del Sr. Sánchez.

5. Dates are formed by using the word "el," the number, the word "de," and the month. For the first day of the month, we use "primero" instead of "uno":

        Hoy es el primero de septiembre.
        Mañana es el tres de agosto.

6.   venir - to come

      vengo   venimos
      viene   vienen

7.   poder - to be able, can

      puedo   podemos
      puede   pueden

8. Like days of the week, months are usually written with a small letter. Again, we often see them capitalized today.

        Mañana es el tres de agosto.
        Es el dieciocho de enero.

CULTURE:

"Está en su casa", ("You are in your house") is a common expression of hosts to a guest in an Hispanic household. The guest should greet the heads of the household first and then the children. He should shake hands with the entire group upon arriving and leaving. Hispanic parents appreciate a guest meeting and talking to their children. They also appreciate compliments about their home. It is customary for a guest to bring flowers. If the purpose of the visit is business, the guest should first discuss family, interests, or subjects not related to the business and later introduce the business discussion. Since our form of government is quite different from that of many Hispanic countries, it is wise to stay away from the subject of politics.

Spanish American houses are usually built close to one another. Many apartments have balconies and houses have patios. Houses are close to the sidewalk and their windows often have wrought iron bars, for decoration but also to discourage burglars. The patio is a yard surrounded by three walls of the house. It affords private outdoor living. City houses usually have modern conveniences such as refrigerators and washing machines, but country or suburban homes may not.

PRACTICE:
1. Prepare two questions to ask other students, using a possessive. Examples: ¿Cómo está el hijo de la señora López? ¿Quién tiene la revista de María?

2. Practice using the verb "gustar" by asking questions of one another. Examples: ¿Le gustan a Ud. las casas grandes o pequeñas? ¿Le gusta a Pepe el béisbol?

3. ¿Cuál es la fecha de hoy? Answer in a complete Spanish sentence:

a. March 30
b. August 4
c. May 1
d. January 2
e. November 29

f. December 15
g. February 20
h. September 10
i. June 11
j. April 18

4. How many rooms are there in your house or apartment? Name them.

5. Tell five activities that you can do around the house.

6. Describe your town or city.

EXTRA VOCABULARY:
al lado de   beside, near
al parecer   apparently
alfombra, la   carpet

almohada, la   pillow
ancho   wide
apartamento, el   apartment
armario, el   closet
artículo, el   article
bosque, el   woods, forest
cama, la   bed
campo, el   field, countryside
cómodo   comfortable
coser   to sew
cucaracha, la   cockroach
edificio de apartamentos, el   apartment house
escuchar   to listen (to)
espejo, el   mirror
estufa, la   stove
garaje, el   garage
habitación, la   room
jugar a los naipes   to play cards
mesa, la   table
moderno   modern
molestar   to annoy
muebles, los   furniture
palacio, el   palace
Pase usted.   Come in.
rascacielos, el   skyscraper
ratón, el   mouse
sábana, la   sheet
silla, la   chair
sillón, el   armchair
sofá, el   sofa
toalla, la   towel
tostador, el   toaster
ventana, la   window

LESSON 7

UN VIAJE

Les gusta mucho su viaje a México.	They like their trip to Mexico a lot.
¿Les gustan a Uds. los viajes largos?	Do you (pl.) like long trips?
Aquí está su pasaporte.	Here is your passport.
No tengo nada que declarar.	I have nothing to declare.
Quisiera cambiar este cheque de viaje.	I would like to cash this traveler's check.
Quisiera el cambio en monedas.	I would like the change in coins.
Ud. puede cambiar su dinero en este banco.	You can change your money in this bank.
El mozo dice, - Por aquí, señor.	The porter says, "This way, Sir."
Esa maleta es pesada.	That suitcase is heavy.
Ese taxi va muy rápido, ¿verdad?	That taxi is going very fast, isn't it?
Llevo mi equipaje desde el aeropuerto al hotel.	I am taking my luggage from the airport to the hotel.
¿Dónde está la estación de ferrocarril?	Where is the railroad station?
¿Cuándo sale el tren para Guadalajara?	When does the train leave for Guadalajara?
¿Cuánto cuesta un billete para Buenos Aires?	How much does a ticket for Buenos Aires cost?
Quisiera un billete de ida y vuelta para La Paz.	I would like a round trip ticket for La Paz.
En primera clase cuesta más que en segunda.	First class costs more than second.

¿De veras?	Really?		
¿Dónde están los servicios?	Where are the toilets?		
Están adelante.	They are straight ahead.		
Están a la izquierda.	They are to the left.		
Están a la derecha.	They are to the right.		
Partimos otra vez en la Vía 12.	We are departing again on Track 12.		

Lleno, por favor.	Fill it up, please.
¿Necesita Ud. aceite?	Do you need oil?
Tengo un carnet de conducir en coche.	I have a driver's license.
Quisiera alquilar un coche.	I would like to rent a car.
Sé conducir muy bien.	I know how to drive very well.

¿Qué distancia hay hasta Bogotá?	How far is it to Bogota?
¿Puedo aparcar mi automóvil aquí?	May I park my car here?
Buscamos un puesto de gasolina o una estación de gasolina.	We are looking for a gas pump or a gas station.

nada	nothing	algo	something
nadie	no one	alguien	someone
nunca	never	siempre	always
ni	nor, neither	o	or

doscientos	200	setecientos	700
trescientos	300	ochocientos	800
cuatrocientos	400	novecientos	900
quinientos	500	mil	1,000
seiscientos	600		

la primavera	spring	el otoño	fall
el verano	summer	el invierno	winter

el día	day
la semana	week
el mes	month
el año	year

EXPLANATION:

1. Gustar - to be pleasing, to like
"Les gusta" and "les gustan" mean "they like" or "you (pl.) like"
Les gusta mucho su viaje a México.   Their trip to Mexico is very pleasing to them.
¿Les gustan a Uds. los viajes largos?   Are long trips pleasing to you (pl.)?

2. In Spanish nouns cannot modify nouns (gasoline station - both words are nouns.)   The two words are joined together with the word "de," (estación de gasolina - station of gasoline):
        Quisiera cambiar este cheque de viaje.
        ¿Donde está la estación de ferrocarril?

3. Adjectives that describe a noun follow the noun:
        Me gustan los edificios altos.
        ¿Les gustan a Uds. los viajes largos?
Other adjectives precede the noun:
        mi pasaporte
        este cheque
        primera clase
        muchos puertorriqueños
        cada día

4. "Quisiera" is a softer way to make a request than "quiero" just as "I would like" is less demanding than "I want":
        Quisiera el cambio en monedas.

5. The words for "this" and "these" are este, esta, estos, and estas.
| este hombre | this man | estos hombres | these men |
| esta mujer | this woman | estas mujeres | these women |

The words for "that" and "those" are ese, esa, esos, and esas.
| ese hombre | that man | esos hombres | these men |
| esa mujer | that woman | esas mujeres | those women |

        Quisiera cambiar este cheque de viaje.
        Esa maleta es pesada.

6. In order to form a negative sentence in Spanish, one must place a negative in front of the verb.   More than one negative is often used in one sentence:

No comprendo.	I don't understand
No tengo nada.	I don't have anything.
El nunca viene.	He never comes.
El no viene nunca.	He never comes.
Nadie sabe cantar.	No one knows how to sing
No sabe cantar nadie.	No one knows how to sing.

7.   ver - to see   saber - to know, to know how

veo	vemos	sé	sabemos
ve	ven	sabe	saben

8. "Querer" (to want, love), "desear" (to want, desire), "saber" (to know, to know how), "poder" (to be able, can) require the infinitive form directly after them when they are followed by a verb:

Miguel quiere ser arquitecto.
Desean comer en seguida.
Sé conducir muy bien.
¿Puedo aparcar mi coche aquí?

("Querer" and "desear" are used interchangeably with the meaning "to want." The first two examples above could have been "Miguel desea ser arquitecto." and "Quieren comer en seguida.")

"Aprender" (to learn) and "ir" (to go) require "a" before the infinitive when they are followed by a verb:

Los niños aprenden a nadar.
Va a llegar a las dos.

CULTURE:

Travel to Spanish America offers tremendous variety and has the advantage of being, in many cases, geographically close to the United States.
Almost all of the countries offer the opportunity of using the Spanish language, and have Spanish culture reflected in their architecture, religion, dance, music, and customs. Visit a small, old city and you will see that it is built around a square (plaza) with,

perhaps, a fountain or a monument, some flowers and/or greenery, and benches. The sides of the plaza may be bordered by a church, perhaps the town hall, and some stores.

There is a huge and spectacular variety of natural beauty; mountains, volcanos, waterfalls, deserts, jungle, beaches, lakes, and farmland (the pampas of Argentina) in Spanish America. Its climate is delightful because of the elevation. Mountains provide relief from the heat of the tropical regions (Mexico, Central America, and parts of South America).

For those seeking a beach resort, there is a vast choice, the islands of the Caribbean, the shores of Mexico, Central America and South America. Many countries offer an Indian flavor, particularly the Andean countries of Peru, Ecuador, and Bolivia. Mexico and northern Central America also have a strong Indian influence.

In the Caribbean , Central America, and northern South America, the culture of the black race is evident in the music and dance.

Some countries offer archeological treasures, such as, the Mayan ruins of Mexico and Guatemala, the Aztec ruins of Mexico, and the Inca ruins of Peru, to name a few.

In some countries the Spanish spectacle of the bullfight is still enjoyed.

European culture is especially prominent in Argentina, whose population, much like ours, is made up of European immigrants (principally Italian and German). Its capital, Buenos Aires, is considered the "Paris" of the American continent.

Consult with a travel agent for the best time to visit specific countries because the climate varies a great deal. During our summer, some of the tropical areas are uncomfortably hot, but, in southern South America it is winter weather.

PRACTICE:

1. Prepare two questions to be answered in a complete sentence in the negative by your fellow students.

2. Prepare a short dialogue on each of the following:
   a. at the airport
   b. at the train station
   c. at the gas station

3. Compose five Spanish sentences using different forms of "this," "these," "that," and "those."

4. Describe the weather in the different seasons. Example: En la primavera hace fresco y llueve mucho.

EXTRA VOCABULARY:
acampar   to camp
además   besides
agencia de viajes, la   travel agency
aire acondicionado, el   air conditioning
antes de   before
asiento, el   seat
¡Buen viaje! Have a good trip!
cámara, la   camera
confirmar   to confirm
costa, la   coast
costar (ue)   to cost
Creo que sí.   I believe so.
delante de   in front of
después de   after
durante   during
estación, la   station
guía turística, la   tourist guide booklet
hacer la maleta   to pack one's suitcase
hacer un viaje   to take a trip
¡Hasta junio, si Dios quiere! See you in June, God willing!
hotel, el   hotel
maleta, la   suitcase
mapa, el   map
peligroso   dangerous
por ejemplo for example
reservación, la   reservation
reservar   to reserve
según   according to
seguro, el   insurance
tren, el   train
turista, el, la   tourist
viaje de negocios, el   business trip
visa, la   visa

LESSON 8

UN RESTAURANTE

HRVICIN 88

¿Tiene Ud. hambre?		Are you hungry?	
Sí, y también tengo sed.		Yes, and I am also thirsty.	
Vamos a un restaurante.		Let's go to a restaurant.	
¿Cuál prefiere Ud.?		Which one do you prefer?	
Me gustan los restaurantes latinos.		I like Latin American restaurants.	
Hay un restaurante mexicano al lado de la biblioteca.		There is a Mexican restaurant next to the library.	
Por favor, tráigame el menú.		Please bring me the menu.	
¿Qué va Ud. a comer?		What are you going to eat?	

la mantequilla	butter	la papa	potato
la confitura	jam	las papas fritas	fried potatoes
el huevo	egg	el arroz	rice
el jamón	ham	los frijoles	beans
el tocino	bacon	la hamburguesa	hamburger
los cornflés	cornflakes	la carne de res	beef
el pan	bread	la carne de cerdo	pork
los panecillos	rolls	el pollo	chicken
el churro	fritter	el chorizo	spicy sausage
el pan tostado	toast	el queso	cheese
el sandwich	sandwich	las legumbres	vegetables
la sopa	soup	las verduras	greens, green
la ensalada	salad		vegetables
la sal	salt	las frutas	fruit
la pimienta	pepper	las naranjas	oranges
el helado	ice cream	las manzanas	apples

45

los pasteles	pastry	las uvas	grapes
el flan	caramel custard	los plátanos	bananas

¡Buen provecho!
Good appetite!

Pues, me gusta mucho arroz con pollo.
Well, I like rice and chicken a lot.

La paella es un plato delicioso.
"Paella" is a delicious dish.

No me gustan los platos muy picantes.
I don't like highly spiced dishes.

¿Qué le gustaría beber?
What would you like to drink?

el agua	water	la limonada	lemonade
el agua mineral	mineral water	el chocolate	chocolate
la leche	milk	el vino	wine
el café	coffee	el vino blanco	white wine
el café negro	black coffee	el vino rojo	red wine
el té	tea	el coctel	cocktail
la Coca Cola	Coca Cola	la cerveza	beer
el jugo de naran_ jas	orange juice		

¡Salud!
To your health!

¿Qué hay de postre?
What is there for dessert?

¿Está incluido el servicio?
Is the service charge included?

una propina por el buen servicio
a tip for the good service

un vaso	a glass	un tenedor	a fork
una botella	a bottle	un cuchillo	a knife
una taza	a cup	una cuchara	a spoon
		una cucharita	a teaspoon

el desayuno	breakfast	la tapa	snack of hors d'oeuvres
el almuerzo	lunch		
la cena	supper	la merienda	afternoon snack
la comida	meal, food	el bocadillo	bite to eat, snack

More "tener" expressions:

tener vergüenza	to be ashamed
tener suerte	to be lucky
tener prisa	to be in a hurry
tener cuidado	to be careful

EXPLANATION:

1. There are two words in Spanish that express the English word "what." "Qué" is used for information or a definition and "cuál" for a selection among more than one option:

¿Qué hay de postre?	information
¿Qué es una "pampa"?	definition
¿Cuál prefiere Ud.?	selection

2. Feminine - words which begin with stressed "a" require the masculine word "el" for "the":

el agua

However, "agua" requires a feminine adjective:

el agua fría

3. To form numbers expressing hundreds, say the number of hundreds, and follow up directly with the next number:

ciento treinta y dos	132
quinientos cinco	505
ochocientos veintinueve	829
novecientos cuarenta y siete	947
setecientos cincuenta y seis	756

"Mil" is used to express the number 1,000:

Tengo mil dólares.	I have a thousand dollars.
mil novecientos ochenta y ocho	1988
mil ochocientos	1800

4. Some verbs change "e" to "ie" and "o" to "ue" in the stem of the verb. The endings are regular. No change is made to the "e" of the "we" form nor the "o" of the "we" form of the verb:

<u>"ar" verbs</u>

empezar - to begin   contar - to count, to tell, relate

empiezo	empezamos	cuento	contamos
empieza	empiezan	cuenta	cuentan

Other verbs of this type are:

encontrar	to find	mostrar	to show
costar	to cost	almorzar	to have lunch
cerrar	to close	pensar	to think
recordar	to remember		

"er" verbs

perder - to lose		volver - to return	
pierdo	perdemos	vuelvo	volvemos
pierde	pierden	vuelve	vuelven

Other verbs of this type are:

entender	to understand	querer	to love, to want
poder	to be able, can		

"ir" verbs

preferir - to prefer		dormir - to sleep	
prefiero	preferimos	duermo	dormimos
prefiere	prefieren	duerme	duermen

Other verbs of this type are:

sentir	to feel	morir	to die

5. hacer - to make, to do   decir - to say, to tell

hago	hacemos	digo	decimos
hace	hacen	dice	dicen

CULTURE:

Spanish American eating habits are a little different from those of the United States. Breakfast is usually taken early in the morning and consists of coffee and bread with butter or jelly. The meal taken in the afternoon between 1:30 and 3:30 is "la comida" or "el almuerzo," a hearty meal similar to our evening dinner, except for dessert, which is usually fruit and cheese, rather than our sweet. In some countries there is a snack, "la merienda" of perhaps a sandwich at 6 o'clock, and, at about 8:00 P.M., "la cena," supper, another full sized meal, only slightly lighter than the main meal.

Again, life is changing, women are entering the work field; traffic is too heavy to allow going home for the mid-day meal; work hours, in some countries, are eliminating the two hour lunch break; and so some Spanish Americans are adopting meals fairly similar to ours.

Different countries have their own foodstuffs depending upon agricultural output. Mexico's main staple is corn, and the tortilla (pancake made from corn meal) is eaten much as we would eat bread. In Argentina, cattle raising is one of the main industries, and barbecued beef is very popular. Rice, beans, and plantains are foods which are plentiful and therefore inexpensive in the Caribbean islands and in a great part of Spanish America.

The food is quite spicy in Latin America.

Most Spanish Americans buy bottled water for drinking water since pure water is not the rule in their countries.

Today, to get the waiter's attention, one raises his hand and calls "señor" or "señorita" rather than the "mozo", "moza" or "camarero", "camarera" of several years ago.

In Spanish American restaurants, there is usually a service charge of 15% on the bill. However, if the restaurant is an expensive, gourmet type and the service is good, it is usual for the customer to leave a little more for an extra tip.

PRACTICE:

1. Draw up a menu for a Mexican restaurant using "pesos" for the prices.

2. Make out a grocery list.

3. Prepare two questions using the verbs which change the stem vowel to ask other students.

4. Give the following numbers in Spanish:
a. 1980   f. 1492
b. 1864   g. 728
c. 630   h. 305
d. 1766   i. 114
e. 501   j. 1227

5. Form groups and prepare a dialogue on food and meals to present to your class. Perhaps two or three of you are going to a restaurant. You might be inviting a friend for lunch or dinner. You may be discussing a third person and her skill or lack of skill in preparing certain dishes. Use your imagination for the situations, and use the vocabulary learned up to now. The various forms of "gustar" would be useful here.

EXTRA VOCABULARY:
adelgazar   to slim down
aguardiente, el   hard liquor
ambiente, el   atmosphere
apetito, el   appetite

azúcar, el   sugar
bistec, el   steak
CABALLEROS   men's room
café, el   cafe
caloría, la   calorie
carne, la   meat
cebolla, la   onion
cocinar   to cook
crema, la   cream
DAMAS   ladies' room
dieta, la   diet
dueño, el   owner
engordar   to get fat, put on weight
estar a dieta   to be on a diet
la cuenta, por favor   the bill, please
pagar   to pay
perro caliente, el   hot dog
pescado, el   fish
picar   to nibble , pick at
plato internacional, el   foreign dish
plato principal, el   main course
precio, el   price
probar (ue)   to taste, to try
rosbif, el   roastbeef
sabor, el   taste, flavor
sangría, la   drink made with red wine and fruit
servicio, el   service
taberna, la   bar
tortilla, la   omelet

IR DE COMPRAS

Mauicir 88

Vamos al centro en autobús.	Let's go downtown by bus.
A mí me gusta más ir en el metro.	I'd rather go by subway.
¿Está lejos la plaza?	Is the square far away?
No, podemos ir a pie en diez minutos.	No, we can walk it in ten minutes.
Está bien.	Okay.
¿Hay muchas tiendas en la plaza?	Are there many stores in the square?
¿Qué quiere Ud. comprar?	What do you want to buy?
Tengo que comprar ropa y también quiero comprar regalos para mis a_ migos en los Estados Unidos.	I have to buy clothes and also I want to buy gifts for my friends in the United States.
Yo también debo comprar algunos regalos.	I, too, should buy some gifts.
Juan compra ropa y Ana compra joyas.	John is buying clothing and Anna is buying jewelry
El compra pantalones y ella compra un anillo	He is buying pants and she buying a ring.
Hay una tienda de ropa en esta es_ quina.	There is a clothing store on this corner.
¿En qué puedo servirle, señor?	May I help you, sir?
Busco zapatos negros.	I am looking for black shoes.
¿Qué tamaño?	What size?
Número diez.	Size 10.
¿Cuánto cuestan?	How much do they cost?
Doce pesos.	Twelve pesos.
¡Ay, son muy caros!	Oh, they are very expensive!
De ninguna manera, son baratos.	Not at all, they are inexpensive

¿Le pago al dependiente? (a la de_
pendienta)
¿O debo pagar en la caja?

Do I pay the salesman? (the
salesgirl)
Or should I pay at the cashier's?

la camisa	shirt	la falda	skirt
el sombrero	hat	las medias	stockings
los calcetines	socks	el suéter, el	sweater
los pantalones	pants	pulóver	
la chaqueta	jacket	las zapatillas	slippers
los zapatos	shoes	los guantes	gloves
el abrigo	overcoat	el pañuelo	handkerchief
el traje de baño	bathing suit	el traje	suit
la ropa interior	underwear	el vestido	dress
las pantimedias	panty hose	el maquillaje	make-up
el sostén	bra	los anteojos	glasses
el cuadro	picture	el libro	book
la pintura	painting	el bolso	purse
la cámara	camera	los aretes	earrings
rojo	red	rosado	pink
anaranjado	orange	purpúreo	purple
amarillo	yellow	moreno	brown
verde	green	blanco	white
azul	blue	negro	black
violeta	violet	gris	gray

EXPLANATION:
1. "Tener que" + infinitive means "to have to" do something:
    Tengo que comprar ropa.

    "Deber" + infinitive means "ought to" do something and implies
somewhat of a moral obligation.
        Yo también debo comprar algunos regalos.

2. The subject pronouns (yo, él, ella, nosotros/as, ellos, ellas) are
used:
a. for emphasis:
        Yo también debo comprar algunos regalos.
b. to avoid confusion:
        El compra pantalones para su hermano y ella
compra un anillo para su madre.

3. To express a command, omit the "o" ending from the "yo" form of the verb and add "e" for the singular and "en" for the plural of verbs that end in "ar." For verbs that end in "er" and "ir," the endings are "a" and "an." The pronouns Ud. and Uds. are used with these command forms.

¡Hable Ud.!	Speak! (one person addressed)
¡Hablen Uds.!	Speak! (more than one person addressed)
¡Coma Ud.!	Eat!
¡Coman Uds.!	Eat!
¡Escriba Ud.!	Write!
¡Escriban Uds.!	Write!
¡Tenga Ud. cuidado!	Be careful!
¡Vengan Uds. al mercado!	Come to the market!
¡Duerma Ud.!	Go to sleep!
¡Vuelva Ud.!	Come back!

4. For the expression "let us" + a verb, use "vamos a" + infinitive:

Vamos a comprar regalos.	Let us buy gifts.
Vamos a comer.	Let us eat.

"Vamos a", when not followed by a verb may mean: let's go, we go, and we are going.

Vamos al centro.	Let's go downtown. We go downtown. We are going downtown.
Vamos al cine el sábado.	We go (are going) to the movies on Saturday. Let's go to the movies on Saturday.

5.

dar - to give		poner - to put	
doy	damos	pongo	ponemos
da	dan	pone	ponen

CULTURE:

One is expected to bargain in a marketplace in Spanish America. Usually the price asked is about twice the value of the merchandise so one can offer about two thirds or less. Tourists are often approached by venders on the street. Bargaining is definitely called for in this situation.   However, the marked prices in a store, particularly a department store or an exclusive shop are realistic, and there should be no question of bargaining.

Spanish Americans, in general, dress up more than people in the United States do.   Little girls wear frilly dresses and dressy little shoes and little boys, suits, shirts, and ties, when going visiting or to a restaurant.   Teenagers now wear jeans and knitted T-shirts, but adults dress more conservatively with somewhat somber colors.

PRACTICE:

1. Ask one another, "¿Qué tiene Ud. que hacer en el centro?"

2. Ask one another the colors of clothing or objects in the classroom. Examples: ¿De qué color es el bolso de _____? (someone in the class) ¿De qué color son los pantalones de _____?

3. Play store.   One person can be the shopkeeper and another the customer.

4. Practice the command form by telling your neighbor to do something.   He, in turn, can show that he understands by performing the action required.

EXTRA VOCABULARY:

almacén, el   department store
anuncio, el   advertisement
bolígrafo, el   ball point pen
carnicería, la   butcher's shop
corbata, la   tie
cuero, el   leather
debajo de   under
detrás de   behind
ganga, la   bargain
gastar   to spend
hacia   toward
impermeable, el   raincoat
lápiz, el   pencil
llevar   to wear, to carry
muñeca, la   doll
necesitar   to need
oro el   gold

panadería, la   bakery shop
perfumería, la   perfume shop
pijamas, los   pajamas
plata, la   silver
poncho, el   poncho, blanket used over shoulders
regatear   to bargain
sobre   on, over
tienda de comestibles, la   grocery shop
vender   to sell
venta, la   sale

LESSON 10

EL CUERPO HUMANO

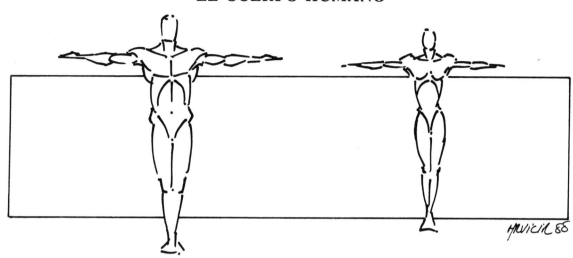

Estoy enfermo: me duele la cabeza.   I am sick: I have a headache.
Me siento débil.   I feel weak.
Tengo dolor de estómago.   I have a stomach ache.
Estoy embarazada.   I am pregnant.
¿A qué hora llega el médico?   What time does the doctor arrive?
Necesito píldoras o medicina.   I need pills or medicine.
Soy alérgico a la penicilina.   I am allergic to penicillin.
El médico pregunta, - ¿Dónde le   The doctor asks, "Where does it
duele?   hurt?"
Me duelen los dientes: ¿dónde hay   My teeth hurt: where is there a
un dentista?   dentist.
¿Puede Ud. preparar esta receta?   Can you fill this prescription?
Tengo que ir al centro para   I have to go downtown to buy
comprar medicina.   medicine
En casa no hay mucha medicina.   There is not much medicine at home.
Pido aspirina en la droguería.   I ask for aspirin at the drugstore.

el pelo	hair	los dedos	fingers
los ojos	eyes	los brazos	arms
la nariz	nose	las nalgas	buttocks
la boca	mouth	las piernas	legs
las manos	hands	los pies	feet
la cara	face	el pecho	chest, bosom
la cintura	waist		

Tengo el pelo moreno.   I have brown hair.
Papá tiene la nariz larga.   Dad has a big nose.

el apéndice	appendix	los vómitos	vomiting
el insomnio	insomnia	el resfriado	cold
los calambres	cramps	el tampón	tampon
la diabetes	diabetes	las toallas higié-nicas	sanitary napkins
la diarrea	diarrhea	el esparadrapo	adhesive tape
la fiebre	fever	el condón	condom
la tos	cough	el termómetro	thermometer
la insolación	sunstroke	la inyección	injection
el aborto	abortion, miscarriage	el yodo	iodine
el SIDA	AIDS		

Sírvase cortarme el pelo	Please give me a haircut.
hacerme la manicura.	give me a manicure.
afeitarme.	give me a shave.
lavarme el pelo.	give me a shampoo.
lavarme y marcarme el pelo.	wash and set my hair.
teñirme del mismo color.	tint my hair the same color.

¿Dónde hay una lavandería?	Where is there a laundry?
¿Dónde hay un teléfono?	Where is there a telephone?
Quiero llamar por teléfono a mi esposa (mi esposo, mi novio, mi novia).	I want to call my wife (my husband, my boyfriend, my girlfriend).
Sírvase marcar el número por mí.	Please dial for me.
Soy extranjero.	I am a foreigner.
¿Cuánto cuesta alquilar un coche para una semana?	How much does it cost to rent a car for a week?
Hola, diga, aló, bueno	Hello (answers to a telephone call)
Quisiera un rollo en color para esta cámara.	I'd like a color film for this camera.

EXPLANATION:

1. In Spanish, the possessive (mi, su, nuestro/a) is seldom used with parts of the body. The word for "the" is used:

Me duele la cabeza.
Tengo el pelo moreno.

2. The word "en" is used for "at" when there is no motion in the sentence. "A" is used with a verb expressing motion:

> En casa no hay mucha medicina.
> Pido aspirina en la droguería.
> Tengo que ir al centro para pedir medicina.

3. "Preguntar" means "to ask" in the sense of asking a question:

> El médico pregunta, -¿Dónde le duele?

"Pedir" means "to ask" in the sense of asking for something.

> Pido aspirina en la droguería.

4.

	salir - to leave
salgo	salimos
sale	salen

5. Some verbs change "e" to "i" in the stem of the verb. The verb endings are regular. No change is made to the "e" in the "we" form.

	servir - to serve
sirvo	servimos
sirve	sirven

Other verbs of this type are:

pedir	to ask for	reír	to laugh
seguir	to follow	vestir	to dress

CULTURE:

Spanish speaking people use their bodies a great deal when they speak. Not only do they use their mouths and facial muscles to pronounce their words more than English speaking people do, but they also move their eyes, hands, their whole stance to emphasize their words. They tend to move their heads quite close to that of the person being spoken to if they are feeling very intense about something. The following are just a few of the gestures used:

1. Fold your hand and stroke your cheek with the fingers of the folded hand.
This movement shows that someone is "polishing the apple," or trying to make a good impression on someone in a superior position.
2. Open your hands and hold them with palms facing you, lift your shoulders, and look at your hands. Means "Of course", "That's obvious".
3. Criss-cross your hands in front of you. "That's it." "That's all there is to it."
4. Hold your index fingers stiff across each other at right angles. "I'll pay you half the price."

5. Put the palm of your hand opposite your face and wiggle your fingers. This gesture means either "hello" or "good-bye."

6. Bunch up your fingers and move them toward your mouth. This demonstrates eating.

7. Place the palm of your left hand over the back of your right hand near the right ear. This indicates sleeping.

PRACTICE:

1. Ask two questions of your classmates about the body. Examples: ¿Dónde está la nariz? ¿Cuántos ojos tiene Ud.?

2. One student is the doctor, another the patient. Prepare a dialogue for this situation.

3. A student asks another to do something for him. The student addressed shows by motions that he understands the request. Examples: Sírvase darme medicina. Sírvase afeitarme.

4. Write two sentences in which you change the "e" to "i" in the stem of the verb. Examples: El camarero nos sirve sopa.   Le pedimos ensalada.

EXTRA VOCABULARY:
accidente, el   accident
¡Ay de mi!   Oh, my!
caminar   to walk
cepillo de dientes, el   tooth brush
collar, el   necklace
corazón, el   heart
¡Cuidado!   Watch out!
desgraciadamente   unfortunately
ejercicio, el   exercise
emergencia, la   emergency
enfermedad, la   illness, sickness
estimar   to estimate, gauge
herida, la   wound, injury
hospital, el   hospital
jabón, el   soap
rodilla, la   knee
Lo siento.   I'm sorry.
músculo, el   muscle
papel higiénico, el   toilet paper

60

pasta dentrífica, la   tooth paste
perder peso   to lose weight
pulsera, la   bracelet
¡Qué lástima!   What a shame!
¡Qué pena!   What a pity! How sad!
reloj (de pulsera), el   wrist watch
respirar   to breathe
riesgo, el   risk
salud, la   health
salvar   to save (a life)
sangre, la   blood
sano   healthy
ser humano, el   human being
siesta, la   nap
síntoma, el   symptom
¡Socorro!   Help!
sufrir   to suffer
¡Uf!   Phew! Ugh!
vida, la   life

LESSON 11

EL CORREO Y EL BANCO

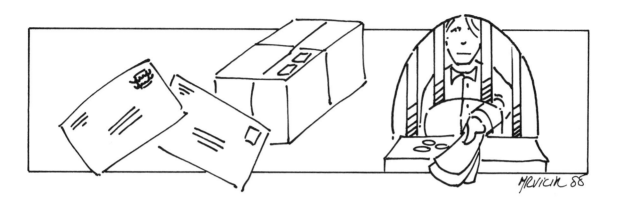

¡Oye, Jesús! ¿Adónde vas?
Hey, Jesus, where are you going?

Voy a la casa de correos para comprar sellos.
I am going to the post office to buy some stamps.

¿Tienes que comprar una tarjeta también?
Do you have to buy a post card, too?

Aquí tienes un paquete postal.
Here is a parcel post package.

Quiero escribirle una carta a mi novia.
I want to write a letter to my girlfriend.

Voy a comprar papel y sobres.
I am going to buy some paper and envelopes.

Después vas a echar tu carta al buzón, ¿verdad?
Later you are going to mail your letter, aren't you?

¡Por supuesto!
Of course!

Tal vez.
Perhaps.

¿Cuánto es el franqueo de una carta para Colombia?
How much is the postage of a letter to Colombia?

No debes mandar dinero sino un giro postal o un cheque.
You should not send money but rather a postal order or a check.

El cartero viene todos los días.
The mailman comes every day.

Si usas el correo aéreo, tu carta va a llegar más temprano.
If you use air mail, your letter will arrive sooner.

Siempre mandamos nuestras cartas por avión.
We always send our letters air mail.

¡Gracias a Dios! Acabo de recibir un cheque de los Estados Unidos.

Thank Heaven! I have just received a check from the United States.

¿Vas a cambiar el cheque en el banco?

Are you going to cash the check in the bank?

Es necesario firmar el cheque en el dorso.

It is necessary to sign the check on the back.

Señor, ¿cómo quiere Ud. el dinero, en billetes de banco o monedas?

Sir, how do you want the money, in bills or in coins?

¿Cuál es el tipo de cambio hoy?

What is the exchange rate today?

Hoy el dólar vale once pesos.

Today the dollar is worth eleven pesos.

Country	Money
Argentina	peso
Bolivia	peso
Canadá	dólar
Chile	peso
Colombia	peso
Costa Rica	colón
Cuba	peso
Ecuador	sucre
El Salvador	colón
España	peseta
Estados Unidos	dólar
Guatemala	quetzal
Honduras	lempira
México	peso
Nicaragua	córdoba
Panamá	dólar
Paraguay	guaraní
Perú	sol
Puerto Rico	dólar
República Dominicana	peso
Uruguay	peso nuevo
Venezuela	Bolívar

EXPLANATION:

1. There is a future tense in Spanish just as there is in English, "hablaré", "I shall speak", etc. but it is simpler to use the verb "ir" + "a" + infinitive to express time in the future:

> ¿Vas a cambiar el cheque en el banco?
> Después vas a echar tu carta al buzón, ¿verdad?

As in English, the present tense is often used to express future time:

¿Vas al cine mañana?	Are you going to the movies tomorrow?
¿Cenas en casa el domingo?	Are you dining at home on Sunday?

2. The word "¿verdad?" at the end of a statement turns the statement into a question and can be translated as "isn't it," "aren't you," "doesn't he," "right?"

Después vas a echar tu carta al buzón, ¿verdad?	Later you're going to mail your letter, aren't you?
Esta lección es muy fácil, ¿verdad?	This lesson is very easy, isn't it?
Juan escribe muchas cartas, ¿verdad?	John writes a lot of letters, doesn't he?

3. Up to now, we have used the formal forms of "you" ("usted" and "ustedes"). The form used among relatives and friends is the familiar "you," "tú" in the singular. The plural is the same form as the formal "you,""ustedes." Add "s" to the "usted" form of the verb to form the singular verb form which is used with "tú." As with the other subject pronouns, except "usted" and "ustedes," "tú" is only used for emphasis. The "s" ending of the verb is enough to show that the familiar "tú" is being used.

> ¿Adónde vas?
> ¿Tienes que comprar una tarjeta postal también?

To express a familiar command, we use the verb form which we have been using with "el," "ella," and "usted":

¡Habla!	Speak!
¡Come!	Eat!
¡Escribe!	Write!
¡Duerme!	Go to sleep!
¡Vuelve!	Come back!

See Lesson 9 for formal commands.

4. There are two words in Spanish that express the English word "where," "dónde" and "adónde."

"Dónde" asks where someone or something is:

>¿Dónde están los hijos?
>
>¿Dónde vive Ud.?

"Adónde" asks where someone or something is going:

>¿Adónde van las niñas?
>
>¡Oye, Jesús! ¿Adónde vas?

5. There is a choice of using or not using the word "the" with certain countries (los Estados Unidos, el Canadá, la Argentina, el Ecuador, el Perú, el Paraguay, el Uruguay). The "El" in El Salvador is a part of the country's name and is always used.

CULTURE:

If you have not exchanged American money for that of the Hispanic country which you are visiting, you can do so at a bank in the airport of your country of destination. If you want to tip before exchanging money, use American currency. The hotel in which you stay will also exchange your money. The best rates are offered at a local bank in the city in which you are staying. Since not all banks exchange money, ask the concierge at your hotel for directions to a bank that does. Carry your passport for identification.

PRACTICE:

1. Ask your fellow students one question having to do with the post office and one, the bank.

2. One person plays the part of a postal clerk (empleado del correo) and another the customer (el cliente). The customer asks three questions of the clerk and the clerk answers.

3. One person plays the part of the bank teller (cajero) and another the customer. The customer asks three questions of the teller and the teller responds.

4. Using the familiar command form, tell someone to perform some action. The student answers the command in pantomime to show that he understands. Examples: ¡Compra un abrigo! ¡Escribe una carta!

5. Form into groups and prepare conversations involving friends who are on a "tú" basis. Subject matter should combine expressions learned in this lesson and those learned in Lesson 7, "Un viaje."

EXTRA VOCABULARY:
a propósito   by the way
abrir una cuenta   to open an account
ahorrar   to save (money)
asegurar   to assure
calculadora, la   calculator
castigo, el   punishment
cheque personal, el   personal check
chequera, la   checkbook
cobrar un cheque   to cash a check
correcto   correct
cortés   polite
Depende.   It depends.
depositar   to deposit
devolver (ue)   to return (give back)
dirección, la   address
distrito postal, el   "Zip" code
Eso es todo.   That's all.
ingresos, los   income
interés, el   interest
llenar   to fill out
ocupado   busy
pedir (i) prestado   to borrow
perder (ie)   to lose
por ciento   percent
préstamo, el   loan
prestar   to lend
problema, el   problem
retirar   withdraw
robar   to rob
robo, el   theft
suma, la   amount
tarjeta de crédito, la   credit card
testigo, el   witness
traducir   to translate

LESSON 12

FIESTAS

Feliz día de santo	Happy Saint's day
Felicitaciones	Congratulations
Feliz cumpleaños	Happy birthday
Feliz Navidad	Merry Christmas
Feliz aniversario	Happy anniversary
Vamos a hacer una fiesta.	Let's have a party.
Invitan a sus mejores amigos.	They invite their best friends.
¿Quién trae el champaña?	Who is bringing the champagne?
Pablo, compra cerveza, por favor.	Paul, please buy beer.
Toman vino rojo y vino blanco.	They are having red wine and white wine.
Vamos al supermercado a mediodía.	We are going to the supermarket at noon.
Debemos tener música.	We should have music.
¿Quién sabe tocar el piano?	Who knows how to play the piano?
Juan, toca la guitarra para nosotros.	John, play the guitar for us.
Raúl tiene muchos discos y cintas.	Ralph has many records and tapes.
Este conjunto sabe muy bien tocar el roc.	This group knows how to play rock very well.
¡Vamos a bailar!	Let's dance.
Vamos a servir palomitas, papas fritas, y sandwiches.	We are going to serve popcorn, potato chips, and sandwiches.

A medianoche nos despedimos de nuestros amigos.	At midnight we say good-bye to our friends.
La corrida de toros empieza a las cuatro.	The bullfight begins at four o'clock.
Me levanto temprano porque no quiero llegar tarde.	I get up early because I do not want to arrive late.
Nos lavamos la cara y nos peinamos.	We wash our faces and comb our hair.
Entonces salimos.	Then we leave.
La gente grita, - ¡Olé! - en la corrida.	People shout, "Bravo!" at the bullfight.
Van a casa en autobús, en el metro, o en coche.	They go home by bus, subway, or car.

acostarse (ue)	to go to bed
bañarse	to take a bath
divertirse (ie)	to have a good time
enojarse	to get angry
lavarse	to wash up
levantarse	to get up
llamarse	to be named
peinarse	to comb one's hair
quedarse	to stay, remain
sentarse (ie)	to sit down

EXPLANATION:

1. The words "tocar" and "jugar" are both translated by "to play" in English. "Tocar" means "to play" a musical instrument:

> ¿Quién sabe tocar el piano?
>
> Juan, toca la guitarra para nosotros.

"Jugar a" means "to play" a game or sport:

> Nos gusta jugar al béisbol.
>
> Jugamos al bridge-contrato.

2. Unlike English, some Spanish verbs require a short pronoun before the conjugated form. The infinitive of these verbs has "se" attached to it (levantarse, peinarse)

> Me levanto temprano.
>
> Nos peinamos.

A chart for the conjugation of "lavarse", "to wash up" is as follows:

(yo) me lavo   (nosotros) nos lavamos
(tú) te lavas
(él) se lava   (ellos) se lavan
(ella) se lava   (ellas) se lavan
Ud. se lava   Uds. se lavan

3. "Nos lavamos la cara." is expressed in English as "We wash our faces." We use the singular form "la cara" because each one of us has only one face. If the sentence were, "We wash our hands.", the Spanish translation would be "Nos lavamos las manos." "Las manos" is plural because we have two hands.

4. Some verbs require the word "de" before an infinitive:

Acabo de recibir un cheque de los Estados Unidos.

As verbs are presented, learn what, if any, prepositions are required before a following infinitive.

CULTURE:

Spanish and Spanish American people love to have a party or a celebration. Most of their fiestas are to celebrate a Catholic holy day, such as Christmas, Easter, or a saint's day. A party can last one day or several days. It usually begins with a tribute to the Catholic person or occasion and may include Mass and perhaps a procession in which a statue is carried on a pedestal on the shoulders of several men. There is plenty of food and drink, music, dancing, and fireworks.

During the summer months in those countries where bullfighting is popular, the fiesta ends with a bullfight. The fans (aficionados) are as deeply involved and as vocal as are our hockey fans. There are three bullfights on a given afternoon, and each bullfight is divided into thirds. During the first third (tercio), the picador, on horseback, drives a hooked lance between the shoulders of the bull. Three banderilleros each drive two colorful, sharply pointed sticks (banderillas) into the bull's neck during the second tercio. And in the third tercio, the true hero of the event, the matador, kills the bull with his sword after first having shown his courage and skilled capework. Most Americans regard bullfighting as cruel and unfair to the animal. The aficionados, however, regard it as an art in which the bullfighter shows his bravery in the face of death.

In remote Indian areas of Spanish America, the fiestas reflect a mixture of Catholicism and the paganism which predates the coming of the Spaniard with his religion. In Caribbean areas the music and dance have an African flavor, which was introduced by the many blacks used as slaves on the sugar cane plantations during the last century.

Spanish speaking people celebrate the date of the birth of the saint for whom they are named, as well as their own birthday.

PRACTICE:

1. Use five of the verbs listed at the end of the vocabulary section in a sentence.

2. Prepare two questions about a party or celebration to ask of your fellow students.

3. Greet a person with one of the expressions presented at the beginning of the vocabulary and follow your greeting with a question or statement.

4. In groups of two or three, prepare a conversation on planning a party, using dates, location, perhaps some vocabulary from Lesson 9, and the vocabulary of this lesson.

EXTRA VOCABULARY:

baile, el   dance
boda, la   wedding
conversar   to converse
copa de champaña, la   glass of champagne
desfile, el   parade
día de fiesta, el   holiday
disfraz, el   costume
divertido   entertaining
excelente   excellent
fuegos artificiales, los   fireworks
gritar   to shout

interesante   interesting
invitación, la   invitation
invitar   to invite
lujoso   luxurious
máscara, la   mask
orquesta, la   orchestra
piñata, la   colorful suspended container made of papier mache
reunión, la   reunion
ron, el   rum
ruido, el   noise
sin duda   no doubt, doubtless
sin embargo   nevertheless
sorprendido   surprised
típico   typical
torta, la   cake

LESSON 13

EL SUPERMERCADO Y EL MERCADO
AL AIRE LIBRE

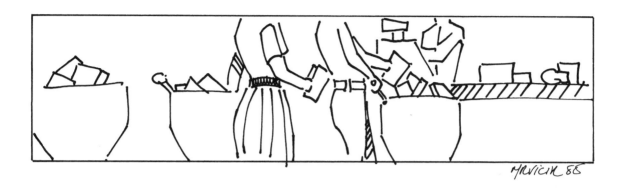

MRVICIK 88

Tenemos tanto dinero como Uds.	We have as much money as you.
Y, por eso, vamos a comprar tantos comestibles como Uds.	And, therefore, we are going to buy as many groceries as you.
¿Dónde hay un supermercado?	Where is there a supermarket?
Juan compra más carne que legum_bres.	John buys more meat than vegetables.
Su amigo compra menos té que café.	His friend buys less tea than coffee.
¿En qué puedo servirle?	May I help you?
Quisiera una lata de guisantes.	I would like a can of peas.
¿Algo más, señora?	Anything else, Madame?
¿Cómo es el pescado hoy?	What is the fish like today?
Está muy fresco, aun más fresco que ayer.	It is very fresh, even fresher than yesterday.
¿Y las verduras?	And the greens?
Son tan frescas como las legumbres.	They are as fresh as the vegetables.
Ambas son recién cogidas del huerto.	Both are freshly picked from the garden.
La torta es más deliciosa que el bizcocho.	The cake is more delicious than the cookie.
¿Cuestan más las nueces que las frutas?	Do nuts cost more than fruit?
Sí, y, por eso, compramos menos nueces que frutas.	Yes, and therefore, we buy fewer nuts than fruit.

¿Ha pagado la cuenta la Sra. Alvarez?	Has Mrs. Alvarez paid the bill?
No he acompañado a nadie al super_ mercado.	I haven't gone to the supermarket with anyone.
Bueno, pero, ¿quién ha visto a Rafael en el supermercado?	Okay, but who has seen Rafael in the supermarket?
¿Quién sabe?	Who knows.
Aquí se puede comprar un poco de todo.	Here one can buy a little of everything.
Sí, hay comida, ropa, batería de co_ cina, platos, cuadros, libros, juguetes, joyas, y muchas otras cosas.	Yes, there is food, clothing, kitchen utensils, dishes, pictures, books, toys, jewelry, and many other things.
En el mercado se regatea para reba_ jar el precio.	In the market one bargains to lower the price.
!Qué lástima! No se puede probar la ropa porque estamos al aire libre.	What a pity! One cannot try on the the clothing because we are outdoors.
¿Cuánto dinero tienes en el bolso (el bolsillo, la cartera)?	How much money do you have in your handbag (pocket, wallet)?
Cien pesos, nada más.	Only one hundred pesos.
Está bien, por lo menos, podemos comprar un paraguas.	Okay, at least we can buy an umbrella.
Oye, mira, por allá hay un letrero que dice, - Aquí se habla inglés.	Hey, look, there is a sign over there which says, "English is spoken here."
¡Estupendo!	Great!

EXPLANATION:

1. In Spanish, comparisons of equality (as much, as many <u>noun</u> as) are expressed with "tanto/a/os/as <u>noun</u> como":

Tenemos tanto dinero como Uds.

Vamos a comprar tantos comestibles como Uds.

"As <u>descriptive word</u> as" is "tan <u>descriptive word</u>" como":

Son tan frescas como las legumbres.

"Frescas" is feminine plural to go with the word "verduras." The adjective, or descriptive word, must always agree with the word it describes.

2. Comparisons of inequality (more, less <u>noun</u> than) are translated into "más, menos <u>noun</u> que":

Juan compra más carne que legumbres.
Su amigo compra menos té que café.

"More, less <u>adjective</u> than" is "más, menos <u>adjective</u> que":

La torta es más deliciosa que el bizcocho.

3. Words that end in "z" change "z" to "c" for the plural"

nuez   nueces
vez   veces

4. There are many past tenses in Spanish but, in this course, we will "get along" with the equivalent of "have, has accompanied, paid, seen" etc. Just as the English form is expressed by a form of "have" and a past participle (formed by the verb plus "ed" in regular English verbs), the Spanish form is expressed by a form of "haber" plus a past participle (formed by adding "ado" or "ido" to the stem of the verb in regular Spanish verbs). Regular verbs in Spanish add "ado" to the stems of verbs that end in "ar" and "ido" to the stems of verbs that end in "er" and "ir":

hablar   hablado   spoken
pagar   pagado   paid
comer   comido   eaten
aprender   aprendido   learned
vivir   vivido   lived
recibir   recibido   received

The following shows the conjugation of the past tense that we will be using:

he hablado   I have spoken
has hablado   you have spoken
(familiar)
ha hablado   he, she has spoken
Ud. ha hablado   you have spoken
(formal)

hemos hablado   we have spoken
han hablado   they have spoken
Uds. han hablado   you have spoken
(familiar and formal plural)

Like English, Spanish has some irregular past participles:

abrir	abierto	opened
decir	dicho	said
escribir	escrito	written
hacer	hecho	done, made
morir	muerto	died
poner	puesto	put
ver	visto	seen
volver	vuelto	returned

5. To translate the indefinite subject "one" into Spanish, use "se" plus the form of the verb that corresponds to the "el," "ella," "Ud." form:

Aquí se puede comprar un poco de todo.

The English translation for this form is "one can buy," "you can buy", or "people can buy" a little of everything

6. The form "ciento" (100) is used in counting but if "100" is followed by a noun or a number higher than 100, "ciento" is shortened to "cien":

Cien pesos, nada más.
Cien mil - 100,000

7. At the end of a line of print or writing, where we use a hyphen in the center of the text to divide a word, in Spanish there is a short line placed at the bottom of the text:

super_   super-
mercado   market

legum_   vege-
bres   tables

As in English, the words are divided only in syllables.

CULTURE:
Millions of Spanish speaking people live throughout the United States. Mexicans have lived in what is now our Southwest for centuries because the area of California, New Mexico, Arizona, Texas, and Colorado was all a part of Mexico until the middle of the nineteenth century. Mexican migrant workers continue to find their way over the Rio Grande River, the northern boundary of Mexico, to find work picking crops in the United States.
Puerto Ricans have been migrating to the United States since the early 1920's. Their small island cannot support its growing

population, and they come principally to New York City in search of work.

In 1959, when Fidel Castro seized leadership of Cuba, thousands of wealthy Cubans fled to Florida. Later, Castro allowed more Cubans to leave the island and there was a vast migration of poor Cubans to Florida. Today, the population of Miami is almost half Hispanic, largely Cuban.

Hispanics have settled in different parts of the United States, but the Southwest, New York City, and Florida have the largest Spanish speaking populations. Although they have had to accustom themselves to our way of life, many have clung to their Latin customs and traditions. In order to interact with this large part of our population, it is helpful and wise to learn their language, temperament, and customs. The people are warm and demonstrative, they love music and dancing, they are exuberant and talkative, and they do not live by the clock. On the other hand, they are formal and conservative in the matter of courtesy and manners and generous in their hospitality.

Some have entered the professions, and others the world of sports and entertainment, but many are stuck in the hard and low paying jobs of picking crops, washing dishes in restaurants, and performing menial jobs in hotels and hospitals.

Like most foreigners, Spanish speaking people sparkle when they are spoken to in their native tongue. They are complimented, and they feel more comfortable and more cooperative, even if the Spanish is far from fluent.

So keep up your good work of studying the Spanish language and culture.

PRACTICE:

1. Compose a sentence using a comparison of equality and one using a comparison of inequality. Examples: Pedro y Carmen son tan simpáticos como Juan y Sara. El coche rojo es más pequeño que el coche negro.

2. Ask two questions of your fellow students using the past tense learned in this lesson. Examples: ¿Has escrito muchas cartas? ¿Quién ha visto a Manuel?

3. Compose two sentences using the indefinite subject "one". Examples: Se paga en la caja. En Puerto Rico se habla español.

4. In groups of two or three, compose a conversation which occurs in a supermarket or an outdoor market. Try to provide variety by bringing in vocabulary learned in former lessons.

EXTRA VOCABULARY:
ayudar   to help
balanza, la   scale
buscar   to look for
calidad, la   quality
centavo, el   cent
de nuevo, otra vez   again
dulce   sweet
hacer cola   to stand in line
largo   long
lata, la   can
libra, la   pound
limpio   clean
lleno   full
mostrador, el   counter
necesario   necessary
paquete, el   package
pesado   heavy
por aquí   around here
precio, el   price
sucio   dirty
todo el mundo, todos   everybody
útil   useful
varios   several

LESSON 14

EL AEROPUERTO

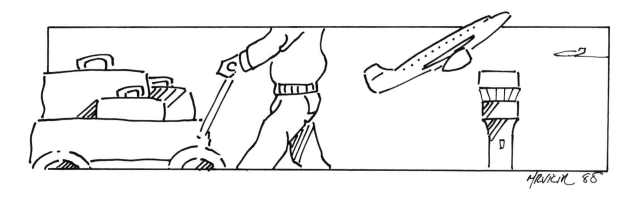

Juan y su esposa están en el aero_
puerto.
Los dos quieren ir al extranjero.
María tiene miedo de ir en avión.
Pero no hay más remedio: para ir a
la Argentina, hay que ir en avión.

Compran los boletos.
Son muy caros porque la Argentina
está muy lejos de los Estados Unidos.

¡Ya lo creo!
Juan y María saben hablar español
pero no conocen a ningún argenti_
no.
No conocen tampoco el país.

Juan va a manejar un carro en
Buenos Aires.
El número de vuelo es Pan American
342. (trescientos cuarenta y dos)
El avión sale de Nueva York a las
diez de la mañana.
Tienen mucho equipaje porque van
a quedarse allá un mes.

John and his wife are at the airport.

Both of them want to go abroad.
Mary is afraid of flying.
But there's nothing anyone can do
about it: in order to go to Argentina
one must fly.
They buy the tickets.
They are very expensive because
Argentina is very far away from the
United States.
I should say so!
John and Mary know how to speak
Spanish but they do not know any
Argentinian.
They are not acquainted with the
country either.
John is going to drive a car in
Buenos Aires.
The flight number is Pan American
342.
The plane leaves New York at 10:00
A.M.
They have a lot of luggage because
they are going to stay there for a
month.

Su equipaje no pesa demasiado.
Está prohibido fumar en esta parte
del avión.
Creo que sí.
La azafata les sirve el almuerzo.
¡Ay, Dios mío!, Juan. Tengo miedo
y estoy enferma.
Pues, querida, ¿por qué no cierras
los ojos y tratas de dormir un poco?
¿Dormir? ¡Ojalá!
Al llegar al aeropuerto en Buenos
Aires, tienen que ir a la aduana.

Muestran los pasaportes y entonces
contestan a algunas preguntas.
Por favor, su nombre.
su nacionalidad
su estado matrimonial
casado, soltero, divorciado
su puerto de salida
su puerto de entrada

Le dan una propina al mozo.
Pepe me da un libro.
Antonio nos muestra el taxi.
Le entrego un plano de la ciudad.

Siempre te digo la verdad.

Their luggage doesn't weigh too much.
Smoking is prohibited in this part
of the plane.
I think so.
The stewardess serves them lunch.
Oh, goodness gracious, John. I am
afraid and I am sick.
Well, darling, why don't you close
your eyes and try to sleep a little?
Sleep? If only I could!
Upon arriving at the airport in
Buenos Aires, they have to go through
customs.
They show their passports and then
answer some questions.
Your name, please.
your nationality
your marital status
married, single, divorced
your port of exit
your port of entry

They give a tip to the porter.
Joe gives me a book.
Anthony shows us the taxi.
I hand him (her, you) a map of the
city.
I always tell you the truth.

EXPLANATION:
1. There are two ways to translate "to know" into Spanish:
"Conocer" means to know a person, place or thing in the sense of being
acquainted with them. It also means to make the acquaintance of some one
The "yo" form is "conozco" and the rest of the verb is regular.

Conocemos a nuestros vecinos.
Conozco a Nueva York.
Mario conoce esa catedral.
Quisiera conocer a tu hermana.

We know our neighbors.
I know New York.
Mario knows that cathedral.
I would like to meet your sister.

"Saber" means to know how to do something or to know a fact.

Juan sabe manejar.   John knows how to drive.

Yo sé que Uds. están de   I know that you are on vacation.
vacaciones.

2. Spanish uses "al" followed by the infinitive to express "upon" doing something:

Al llegar al aeropuerto en Buenos Aires, ...

3. The words "me" - to me, "te" - to you (familiar), "le" - to him, to her, to you (formal), "nos" - to us, and "les" - to them, to you (plural) are usually placed before the conjugated form of the verb. The word "to" is not always expressed in English.

La azafata les sirve el almuerzo.
Te digo la verdad.

"Le" and "les" are used even if the person is mentioned:

Le dan una propina al mozo.

In English "to the porter" suffices but, in Spanish, "le" is used in addition to "al mozo."

CULTURE:

Major cities of Spanish America can be reached by airplane. If one chooses to travel on a foreign line, the trip will start on the airplane since the personnel will be mostly bilingual, Spanish and English, and the food served on board indigenous to the country of the airplane's origin. Upon landing, you can take a taxi to your hotel, or less expensively, a bus. Or you can rent a car.

Public transportation within the large cities is usually inexpensive and widely used since owning a car is not the norm in most Spanish American countries. Buses are the most common means of transportation and, in many capitals, there are subways. Taxis may be more expensive during the evening hours than during the day. If the taxi does not have a meter, ask the fare before you get into the taxi.

If you decide to take a day trip into the countryside, take a train. They are not always modern nor always on time, but riding the trains may be easier for you than driving a rented car. Your hotel may provide tours for groups within the city or in the outlying area.

If you decide to visit an ancient ruin or one of nature's hidden wonders, you may find yourself on a horse or mule for the last part of the trip.

Be sure to drink bottled water, cooked vegetables, and fruit that you can peel or you may find yourself fighting diarrhea.

PRACTICE:

1. Prepare a sentence using "saber" and one using "conocer." Examples: En esta clase todos saben hablar inglés y español. Nunca he conocido a tu novio.

2. Compose two sentences to ask of your fellow students which require a response of "to me, you, him, etc. Examples: ¿A quién le das una propina? Le doy una propina al mozo. ¿Me entrega Ud. una cuenta? Sí, le entrego una cuenta.

3. Describe a trip to some Spanish American destination. Use your large Spanish vocabulary!

4. In groups of two, prepare a conversation in which one is the questioner and the other answers. Perhaps one is the customs agent and the other the passenger or one might be the tourist and the other the stewardess. Again, use your imagination.

EXTRA VOCABULARY:
a bordo de   on board
abrochar el cinturón   to fasten the seatbelt
aeromozo, el   steward
agencia de viajes, la   travel agency
ayudar   to help
bebida gratuita, la   free drink
boleto de primera clase, el   first class ticket
boleto de turista, el   tourist class ticket
¡Cálmate!   Calm down!
capitán, el   captain
contra   against
durar   to last
entre   between
esperar   to wait
fumar   to smoke
internacional   international
línea aérea, la   airline
llegada, la   arrival
maleta, la   suitcase
molestar   to annoy
motor, el   motor

pasajero, el   passenger
piloto, el   pilot
pista, la   runway
rápido   rapid, rapidly
sala de espera, la   waiting room
salida, la   departure
subir   to board
volar (ue)   to fly

LESSON 15

LAS DIVERSIONES

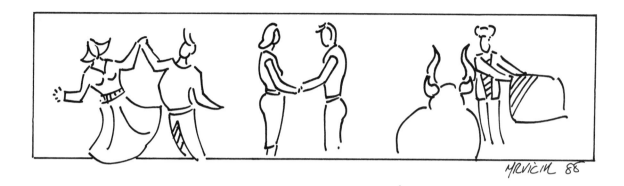

MRVICIN 88

Pedro ha invitado a Elena a salir
con él.
¿Quieres salir conmigo, Elena?

Encantada, ella contesta.
¿Adónde quieres ir?
Pues, como sabes, me gusta mucho
bailar.
A mí me gusta mucho el teatro y a ti
te gusta bailar.
Podemos ir al teatro primero y en_
tonces a un club o a una discoteca,
¿está bien?
Sí, mi amor, siempre me divierto
cuando salgo contigo.
Pedro y Elena están enamorados
y piensan casarse en junio.
Bueno, te veo a las siete en punto.
Hasta luego, Pedro.

José le ha pedido a Susana a pasar
la tarde con él.
Hola, Susana, ¿qué hace Ud. hoy?

No estoy segura. Puesto que no
tengo cita, voy a mirar la televisión.
Se puede mirar la tele en cualquier
día.

Peter has invited Helen to go out
with him.
Would you like to go out with me,
Helen?
I'd be delighted, she answers.
Where do you want to go?
Well, as you know, I like to dance
a lot.
I like the theater a lot and you like
to dance.
We can go to the theater first and
and then to a club or a disco, is that
okay?
Yes, sweetheart, I always have a
good time when I go out with you.
Peter and Helen are in love and
they plan to be married in June.
All right, I'll see you at seven sharp.
See you later, Peter.

Joseph has asked Susan to spend the
afternoon with him.
Hello, Susan, what are you doing
today?
I'm not sure. Since I don't have a
date, I'm going to watch television.
One can watch T.V. any day.

Hoy hace buen tiempo.	It's a nice day today.
¿Quiere Ud. jugar al tenis o al golf?	Would you like to play tennis or golf?
Lo siento. No juego ni al tenis ni al golf.	I'm sorry. I don't play tennis nor golf.
¿Le gustaría ir a un juego de béisbol o a una corrida de toros?	Would you like to go to a baseball game or a bullfight.
No me gusta la corrida porque es tan cruel, pero un juego de béisbol sí que me gusta.	I don't like the bullfight because it is so cruel, but I <u>do</u> like a baseball game.
Dos novios miran la televisión.	Two sweethearts are watching television.
¿Quién ha puesto la tele?	Who put the T.V. on?
Mi hermanito.	My kid brother.
¡Tu hermanito! ¿A él le gustan las telenovelas?	Your little brother! Does <u>he</u> like soaps?
¡Cállate! Ese rubio guapo abraza a su novia. Se besan.	Be quiet! That handsome blond is hugging his girlfriend. They're kissing.
A propósito, Bárbara, ¿dónde está la cerveza?	By the way, Barbara, where is the beer?
Como de costumbre, en la nevera.	As usual, in the refrigerator.
¿Puedo cambiar el canal? Quiero oír las noticias.	May I change the channel? I want to hear the news.
En diez minutos, no más.	In just ten minutes.
¿Puedo tomar otra cerveza?	May I have another beer?
Claro.	Of course.
Más tarde.	Later.
¡Caramba, Tomás! Estás borracho.	Gosh, Thomas, you're drunk!

EXPLANATION:
1. "Mí, ti, él, ella, usted, nosotros, ellos, ellas, ustedes" are used after a preposition (a, de, con, en, para, sobre, etc.):

> Pedro le ha invitado a Elena a salir con él.
> A mí me gusta mucho el teatro.

"Conmigo" - with me, and "contigo" - with you (familiar) are exceptions:

> ¿Quieres salir conmigo, Elena?
> Siempre me divierto cuando salgo contigo.

2. "A" used with the above pronouns is redundant and gives more importance to the pronoun:

> ¿Tu hermanito? ¿A él le gustan las telenovelas?
> A mí me gusta mucho el teatro y a ti te gusta bailar.

3. "Ito, ita" when added to a noun mean "little":

> el hermanito   the little brother

They may also denote affection:

> Te quiero, abuelita. I love you, Grandma.

4. The expression "sí que" placed before the verb is translated into English by "I do" or "I really do":

> Sí que me gusta un juego de béisbol.

5. Certain words which use the word "a" or "an" in English, do not require them in Spanish:

> ¿Puedo tomar otra cerveza?

Other such words are:

cien	Tiene cien dólares.	He has a hundred dollars.
medio	Mamá necesita me_ dia docena de huevos.	Mom needs a half dozen eggs.
cierto	Cierta persona siempre llega tarde.	A certain person always arrives late
mil	Ha cantado esa can_ ción mil veces.	He has sung that song a thousand times.
¡qué!	¡Qué libro! ¡Es mag_ nífico!	What a book! It's great!
sin	Pedro siempre llega sin sombrero.	Peter always arrives without a hat.
tal	Nunca ha visto tal cosa.	He has never seen such a thing.

6. "Se" often means "each other or "to one another":

> Se besan.   They're kissing (each other).

"Nos" can also mean "each other" or "to one another":

> Nos escribimos a menudo   We write to one another often.

CULTURE:

In the area of dating, as in other aspects of culture, things are changing. However, among many Hispanics, there is still more conservatism than among people in the United States. Some parents require their daughters to be accompanied on a date by a younger sister, an aunt, or perhaps a family friend. Engagements are apt to last several years. Marital sex is just that, after marriage.

Young people usually go about in groups rather than as twosomes. Sometimes they gather around a table in a café and chat or play word games. Or they may go to someone's home and play records or tapes and dance. Perhaps they will go to the beach or to a ball game in a group. There are no minimum age requirements for buying alcoholic beverages in Hispanic countries but, more often than not, young people drink coffee or soft drinks.

PRACTICE:

1. Invite someone to go someplace with you. Be specific about when and where.

2. Make up two sentences in which you use one of the following words in each: cien, cierto, medio, mil, otro, ¡qué!, sin, and tal. Example: Pablo tiene mil ideas pero no hace nada.

3. Ask two questions of your fellow classmates in which you use "a" plus a pronoun studied in #1 of the Explanation section of this lesson. Example: ¿A ti te gusta la cerveza?

4. Three or four people get together and discuss plans for a group get-together - where, at what time, food, activities, etc.
or
     Two people get together and plan a date.

EXTRA VOCABULARY:
abrazo, el   hug
actividad, la   activity
amistoso   friendly
asistir a   to attend
baile, el   dance
beso, el   kiss
canción, la   song
cariñoso   affectionate
celoso   jealous
delgado   slender

deporte, el sport
descanso, el rest
entretener to entertain
equipo, el team
esquiar to ski
estar de buen humor to be in a good mood
fin de semana, el week-end
flaco skinny, thin
gordo fat
magnetoscopio, el VCR
Me alegro. I'm glad.
nadar to swim
número de teléfono, el telephone number
para siempre forever
pasatiempo, el pastime, hobby
película, la film, movie
piscina, la pool
playa, la beach
practicar to practice
radio, el radio set
radio, la radio
sinvergüenza, el, la scoundrel
tertulia, la informal social gathering
vacaciones, las vacation
videocasette, el video tape

VOCABULARY SPANISH-ENGLISH

This vocabulary includes all of the Spanish words used in the book with the exception of proper nouns, subject pronouns, object pronouns, and numbers. Verbs are presented only in the infinitive form unless they have a special use, such as "quisiera," etc. Vowel changes in verbs are indicated by the spelling change within parentheses immediately following the verb. Adjectives are presented in the masculine singular form. The definite article follows the noun to indicate gender. Abreviations used are f- feminine, m- masculine, fam.- familiar, and form.- formal.

A

a   to, at
abierto   open, opened
abogado, el   abogada, la   lawyer
a bordo de   on board
aborto, el   miscarriage, abortion
abrazar   to hug, to embrace
abrazo, el   hug
abrigo, el   coat
abrir   to open
abrir una cuenta   to open an account
abrochar el cinturón   to fasten the seat belt
abuela, la   grandmother
abuelita, la   grandma
abuelo, el   grandfather
abuelos, los   grandparents
acabar de   to have just
acampar   to camp
accidente, el   accident
aceite, el   oil
acompañar   to accompany
acostarse (ue)   to go to bed
actividad, la   activity

actor, el   actor
actriz, la   actress
adelante   forward, ahead
adelgazar   to slim down
además   besides
adiós   good-by
¿adónde?   where (motion involved)
aduana, la   customs
aeromozo, el   steward
aeropuerto, el   airport
afeitarse   to shave
agencia de viajes, la   travel agency
agradable   pleasant
agua (f), el   water
agua mineral (f), el   mineral water
aguardiente, el   hard liquor
ahora mismo   right now
ahorrar   to save (money)
aire acondicionado   air conditioned
aire libre, el   open air, outdoors
¡ajá!   aha!
al aire libre   outdoors, in the open air
al contrario   on the contrary

al extranjero abroad
al lado de beside, near
al parecer apparently
al principio at first
a la vez at the same time
alérgico allergic
alfombra, la rug
algo something, anything
alguien someone, somebody
alguno some, any
algunos some, a few
allá there
almacén, el department store
almohada, la pillow
almuerzo, el lunch
¡Aló! Hello! (telephone)
alquilar to rent
alto tall, high
ama (f) de casa, el
housewife
amarillo yellow
ambiente, el atmosphere
ambos both
a mediodía at noon
a medianoche at midnight
a menudo often
amiga, la (f) friend
amigo, el (m) friend
amor, el love
anaranjado orange (color)
ancho wide
anillo, el ring
aniversario, el anniversary
anoche last night
anteojos, los glasses
antes de before
anuncio, el advertisement
año, el year
aparcar to park
apartamento, el apartment
apéndice, el appendix
apetito, el appetite
a pie on foot, walking

aprender to learn
a propósito by the way
aquí here
arete, el earring
armario, el closet
arquitecto, el, arquitecta, la
architect
arroz, el rice
artículo, el article
artista, el, la artist
asegurar to assure
así, así so, so (all right)
asiento, el seat
aspirina, la aspirin
atrás backward, behind
astronauta, el, la astronaut
autobús, el bus
automóvil, el automobile
autopista, la highway
A ver. Let's see.
avión, el airplane
¡ay! oh!
¡Ay de mí! Oh, my!
ayer yesterday
ayudar to help
azafata, la stewardess
azul blue
azúcar, el sugar

B

bailar to dance
baile, el dance
balanza, la scale
banco, el bank
baño, el bath, bathroom
bañarse to take a bath
barato cheap, inexpensive
barbero, el barber
¡Basta! That will do!
batería de cocina, la kitchen
utensils
beber to drink

bebida gratuita, la free drink

béisbol, el baseball

besar to kiss

beso, el kiss

biblioteca, la library

bien well

¡Bienvenido! Welcome!

billete, el ticket, bill (paper money)

billete de banco, el paper money

billete de ida y vuelta, el two way ticket

bistec, el steak

bizcocho, el cookie

blanco white

boca, la mouth

bocadillo, el snack

boda, la wedding

boleto de primera clase, el first class ticket

boleto de turista, el tourist class ticket

boleto, el ticket

bolígrafo, el ball point pen

bolsillo, el pocket

bolso, el purse, handbag

borracho drunk

bosque, el woods, forest

botella, la bottle

brazo, el arm

bridge-contrato, el bridge (card game)

¡Buen provecho! Good appetite!

¡Buen viaje! Have a good trip!

bueno good, okay

¡Bueno! Hello (telephone)

buscar to look for

buzón, el mailbox

C

cabeza, la head

cada each, every

café, el coffee, café

café negro, el black coffee

caja, la box

calambres, los cramps

calcetines, los socks

calculadora, la calculator

calendario, el calendar

calidad, la quality

callarse to be quiet

calle, la street

¡Cálmate! Calm down!

calor, el heat

caloría, la calorie

cama, la bed

cámara, la camera, room

camarera, la waitress

camarero, el waiter

cambiar to change

cambiar un cheque to cash a check

cambio, el change, small change

caminar to walk

camisa, la shirt

campo, el field, countryside

canal, el channel

canción, la song

cansado tired

capitán, el captain

cara, la face

¡caramba! gosh!

cariñoso affectionate

carne, la meat

carne de cerdo, la pork

carne de res, la beef

carnet de conducir, el driver's license

carnicería, la butcher's shop

caro expensive, dear

carpintero, el carpenter
carretera, la highway
carro, el car
carta, la letter
cartera, la wallet
cartero, el mailman
casa, la house
casa de correos, la post office
a casa home (after a verb of motion)
en casa at home
casado married
casarse to get married
casi almost
castigo, el punishment
catedral, la cathedral
cebolla, la onion
celoso jealous
cena, la evening meal
centavo, el cent
centro, el center, downtown
cepillo de dientes, el toothbrush
cerca de near
cerrar (ie) to close
cerveza, la beer
cielo, el sky
cierto certain, sure
cine, el movies, movie theater
cinta, la tape
cinturón de seguridad, el seat belt
cita, la date, appointment
ciudad, la city
claro of course
clase, la class
cliente, el/la client, customer
clima, el climate
club, el club
cobrar un cheque to cash a check
coche, el car

cocina, la kitchen
cocinar to cook
cocinero, el cook
coctel, el cocktail
cogido picked
color, el color
collar, el necklace
comedor, el dining room
comer to eat
comestibles, los food, groceries
comida, la food, meal
como as, like
¿cómo? how
cómodo comfortable
compañero/a de cuarto, el, la roommate
compañía, la company
comprar to buy
con with
condón, el condom
conducir to drive
confirmar to confirm
confitura, la jam
conjunto, el pop group
conmigo with me
conocer to know, be acquainted with, meet (for the first time)
contento happy, contented
contestar to answer
contigo with you (fam.)
contra against
conversar to converse
copa de champaña, la glass of champagne
corazón, el heart
corbata, la tie
cornflés, los cornflakes
correcto correct
correo aéreo, el air mail
correo, el mail
correr to run

corrida de toros, la   bullfight
cortar   to cut
cortés   polite
cosa, la   thing
coser   to sew
costa, la   coast
costar (ue)   to cost
creer   to believe
crema, la   cream
Creo que sí.   I believe so.
cruel   cruel
cuadro, el   picture
¿cuál?   which (one)
cualquier   any at all
cuando   when
¿cuándo?   when
¿cuánto?   how much
¿cuántos?   how many
cuarto   quarter, fourth part
cuarto, el   room
cucaracha, la   cockroach
cuchara, la   spoon
cucharita, la   teaspoon
cuchillo, el   knife
cuenta, la   bill
cuero, el   leather
cuerpo, el   body
¡Cuidado!   Watch out!
cuidado, el   care, concern
cumpleaños, el   birthday
cuñada, la   sister-in-law
cuñado, el   brother-in-law
cura, el   priest

CH

champaña, el   champagne
chaqueta, la   jacket
charlar   to chat
cheque, el   check
cheque de viaje, el
traveler's check

cheque personal, el
personal check
chequera, la   checkbook
chica, la   young girl
chico, el   young boy, guy
chocolate, el   chocolate
chorizo, el   pork sausage
churro, el   fritter

D

dama, la   lady
dar   to give
de   of, from
de costumbre   usually, usual
de nuevo   again
de veras   really
de vez en cuando   from time
to time
debajo de   under
deber   must, ought to
débil   weak
decir   to say, tell
declarar   declare
dedo, el   finger
delante de   in front of
delgado   slender
delicioso   delicious
demasiado   too much
dentista, el, la   dentist
Depende.   It depends.
dependienta, la   clerk, shop
assistant
dependiente, el   clerk, shop
assistant
deporte, el   sport
depositar   to deposit
derecha, la   the right side
derecho, el   right (privilege)
desayuno, el   breakfast
descansar   to rest
descanso, el   rest
desde   from

desear   to want, desire
desfile, el   parade
desgraciadamente
unfortunately
despacio   slowly
despedir (i)   to fire
despedirse de (i)   to say
goodbye, take one's leave
después   afterwards, later
después de   after
detective privado, el
private detective
detrás de   behind
devolver (ue)   to return (give
back)
día, el   day
día de fiesta, el   holiday
día de santo, el   Saint's day
día de trabajo, el   workday
diabetes, la   diabetes
diarrea, la   diarrhea
dicho   said
diente, el   tooth
dieta, la   diet
difícil   difficult
¡diga!   hello! (telephone)
¿Dígame?   Pardon me. (I
didn't hear you.)
diligente   diligent
dinero, el   money
Dios   God
¡Dios mío!   my goodness!
diplomático/a el, la
diplomat
dirección, la   address
disco, el   record
discoteca, la   disco,
discotheque
disfraz, el   costume
distrito postal, el   "Zip code"
diversión, la   amusement,
entertainment, hobby
divertido   entertaining

divertimiento, el
amusement, entertainment
divertirse (ie)   to have a
good time
divorciado   divorced
dólar, el   dollar
doler (ue)   to hurt, pain
¿dónde?   where
dormir (ue)   to sleep
dormitorio, el   bedroom
dorso, el   back
los dos   both
droguería, la   drugstore
dueño, el   owner
dulce   sweet
durante   during
durar   to last

E

echar una carta al buzón   to
mail a letter
edificio, el   building
edificio de apartamentos, el
apartment house
eficiente   efficient
ejercicio, el   exercise
embarazada   pregnant
emergencia, la   emergency
emfermero/a, el, la   nurse
empezar (ie)   to begin
empleado/a el, la   employee
empleo, el   job
en   in, on
en punto   sharp
en vez de   instead of
Encantado.   Delighted.
enfadado   angry
enfermedad, la   illness,
sickness
enfermo   sick
engordar   to get fat, put on
weight

enojarse   to become angry
ensalada, la   salad
enseñar   to teach
entender (ie)   to understand
entonces   then
entrada, la   entrance, entry
entre   between, among
entregar   to hand over
entretener   to entertain
equipaje, el   luggage
equipo, el   team
escribir   to write
escrito   written
escuchar   to listen (to)
escuela, la   school
ese, esa   that
¡Eso es!   That's right!
Eso es todo.   That's all.
esos, esas   those
esparadrapo, el   adhesive
tape
espejo, el   mirror
esperar   to wait, hope
esposa, la   wife
esposo, el   husband
esquiar   to ski
estación, la   season, station
estación de ferrocarril, la
railroad station
estación de gasolina, la   gas
service station
estado, el   state
estar   to be
estar a dieta   to be on a diet
estar de buen humor   to be
in a good mood
estar de vacaciones   to be on
vacation
estar enamorado de   to be in
love with
este, esta   this
estimar   to estimate, gauge
estómago, el   stomach

estos, estas   these
estudiante, el, la   student
estudiar   to study
estufa, la   stove
estupendo   wonderful, great
excelente   excellent
extranjero   foreign

F

fácil   easy
falda, la   skirt
familia, la   family
famoso   famous
fantástico   fantastic
farmacia, la   pharmacy
favor, el   favor
favorito   favorite
fecha, la   date
¡Felicitaciones!
Congratulations!
feliz   happy
feo   ugly
fiebre, la   fever
fiesta, la   party, holiday
fin de semana, el   weekend
firmar   to sign
flaco   skinny, thin
flan, el   carmelized custard
fracaso, el   failure
franqueo, el   postage
fresco   cool, fresh
frijol, el   bean
frío   cold
frutas, las   fruit
fuegos artificiales, los
fireworks
fumar   to smoke

G

ganar   to earn, win
ganga, la   bargain

garaje, el   garage
gaseosa, la   carbonated drink
gastar   to spend
gato, el   cat
gente, la   people
giro postal, el   money order
gordo   fat
gracias   thank you
gracias a Dios   thank Heaven
grande   large
gris   gray
gritar   to shout
guante, el   glove
guapo   handsome, good-looking
guía turística, la   tourist guide booklet
guisante, el   pea
guitarra, la   guitar
gustar   to be pleasing to, to like
¿le gustaría?   would you (form.) like?
gusto, el   pleasure, taste
El gusto es mío.   My pleasure.

H

habilidad, la   skill, ability
habitación, la   room
hablar   to talk, speak
hacer   to make, do
hacer cola   to stand in line
hacer la maleta   to pack one's suitcase
hacer un viaje   to take a trip
hacer una fiesta   to have a party
hacia   toward
hambre, (f), el   hunger
hamburguesa, la   hamburger
hasta   until
hasta luego   see you soon

hasta mañana   see you tomorrow
hay   there is, there are
hay que   one must, it is necessary to
hecho   done, made
helado, el   ice cream
herida, la   wound, injury
hermana, la   sister
hermanito, el   little brother
hermano, el   brother
hermanos, los   brothers, brothers and sisters
hermoso   beautiful, lovely
hielo, el   ice
hija, la   daughter
hijo, el   son
hijos, los   children
hola   hello
¡hola!   hello (telephone)
hombre, el   man
hombre de negocios, el   business man
hora, la   hour, time
hospital, el   hospital
hotel, el   hotel
hoy en día   nowadays
hoy   today
huerto, el   vegetable garden
huevo, el   egg
humano   human

I

iglesia, la   church
igualmente   the same to you, likewise
impermeable, el   raincoat
importante   important
incluido   enclosed, included
ingeniero, el   engineer
ingresos, los   income
insolación, la   sunstroke**

insomnio, el   insomnia
interés, el   interest
interesante   interesting
internacional   international
invierno, el   winter
invitación, la   invitation
invitar   to invite
inyección, la   injection
ir   to go
ir de compras   to go shopping
ir en avión   to fly, go by plane
izquierda, la   the left side

J

jabón, el   soap
jamón, el   ham
jardín, el   garden
jefa, la   boss, manager
jefe, el   boss, manager
joven   young
joyas, las   jewelry
juego, el   game
jugar   to play
jugar a los naipes   to play cards
jugar al golf   to play golf
jugar al tenis   to play tennis
jugo de naranjas, el   orange juice
juguete, el   toy

L

lado, el   side
al lado de   beside, near
lápiz, el   pencil
largo   long
lástima, la   pity
lata, la   can
lavadora, la   washing machine
lavandería, la   laundry
lavar   to wash

lavarse   to wash oneself
lección, la   lesson
leche, la   milk
leer   to read
legumbre, la   vegetable
lejos   far
letrero, el   sign
levantarse   to stand up, to get up
libra, la   pound
libro, el   book
limonada, la   lemonade
limpiar   to clean
limpio   clean
línea aérea, la   airline
loco   crazy, mad
luego   then, next
lujoso   luxurious
luna de miel, la   honeymoon

LL

llamarse   to be named
llegada, la   arrival
llegar   to arrive
llenar   to fill out
lleno   full
llevar   to carry, wear
llover (ie)   to rain
lloviendo   raining
llueve   it is raining
lluvia, la   rain

M

madre, la   mother
magnetoscopio, el   VCR
mal   badly, poorly
maleta, la   suitcase
malo   bad
mañana   tomorrow
mañana, la   the morning
mandar   to send

manejar   to drive
manera, la   way, manner
mano, la   hand
mantequilla, la   butter
manzana, la   apple
mapa, el   map
maquillaje, el   make-up
maravilloso   marvelous
marcar el número   to dial the number
marcar el pelo   to set hair
más   more
más que nunca   more than ever
más tarde   later
máscara, la   mask
matrimonial   marital
matrimonio, el   married couple
Me alegro.   I'm glad.
mecánico, el   mechanic
medianoche, la   midnight
a medianoche   at midnight
medias, las   stockings
medicina, la   medicine
médico, el   doctor
medio   half
mediodía, el   noon
a mediodía   at noon
mejor   better
menos   less
menú, el   menu
mercado, el   market
merecer   to deserve
merienda, la   late afternoon snack
mes, el   month
mesa, la   table
metro, el   subway
mí   me
mi, mis   my
miedo, el   fear
mimado   spoiled

minuto, el   minute
mirar   to look (at)
moderno   modern
mojado   wet
molestar   to annoy
moneda, la   currency
moreno   brown, dark
morir (ue)   to die
mostrador, el   counter
motor, el   motor
moza, la   waitress, servant
mozo, el   servant, waiter, porter
mucho   much, a lot of
muchos   many
muebles, los   furniture
muerto   dead
mujer, la   woman
muñeca, la   doll
músculo, el   muscle
música, la   music
muy   very

N

nacionalidad, la   nationality
nada   nothing
nadar   to swim
nadie   no-one, nobody
nalgas, las   buttocks
naranja, la   orange
nariz, la   nose
necesario   necessary
necesitar   to need
negocios, los   business
negro   black
nevando   snowing
nevar (ie)   to snow
nevera, la   refrigerator
ni   nor
ni.....ni   neither.....nor
nieta, la   grandaughter
nieto, el   grandson

nieva   it is snowing
ninguno   none, not any, no
niña, la   little girl
niño, el   little boy
niños, los   little boys, little children
no   no
¡No me digas!   You don't say!
no más   only
noche, la   night
nombre, el   name
noticias, las   news
novia, la   girlfriend
novio, el   boyfriend
nuera, la   daughter-in-law
nuestro   our
nuevo   new
nuez, la   nut
número, el   number
número de teléfono, el   telephone number
nunca   never

O

o   or
ocupado   busy
oficina, la   office
oficio, el   job, profession, occupation
oír   to hear
¡ojalá!   Let's hope so!
ojo, el   eye
¡olé!   Bravo!
orgulloso   proud
oro, el   gold
orquesta, la   orchestra
otoño, el   autumn, fall
otra vez   again
otro   other

P

padre, el   father
padres, los   parents
paella, la   Spanish dish with rice, shellfish, etc.
pagar   to pay
país, el   country
pájaro, el   bird
palacio, el   palace
palomitas, las   pop corn
pan, el   bread
pan tostado, el   toast
panadería, la   bakery shop
panecillos, los   rolls
pantalones, los   pants, trousers
pañuelo, el   handkerchief
papa, la   potato
papas fritas, las   (French) fried potatoes, potato chips
papel higiénico, el   toilet paper
papel, el   papel
paquete, el   package
paquete postal, el   parcel post package
para   for, in order to
para siempre   forever
paraguas, el   umbrella
pariente, el   relative
parte, la   part
partir   to depart
pasajero, el   passenger
pasaporte, el   passport
pasar   to spend time, to happen
pasatiempo, el   pastime, hobby
Pase usted.   Come in.
pasta dentrífica, la   tooth paste
pastel, el   pastry

patio, el patio, courtyard
pedir (i) to ask (for something), to request
pedir (i) prestado to borrow
peinarse to comb one's hair
película, la film, movie
peligroso dangerous
pelo, el hair
peluquería, la hairdresser's, barber shop
peluquero, el hairdresser
penicilina, la penicillin
pensar (ie) to think, intend to
pequeño small
perder (ie) to lose
perder (ie) peso to lose weight
perdón excuse me
perfumería, la perfume shop
periódico, el newspaper
periodista, el, la journalist
permiso, el permission
pero but
persona, la person
perro, el dog
perro caliente, el hot dog
pesado heavy
pesar to weigh
pescado, el fish
peso, el monetary unit
piano, el piano
picante hot, highly seasoned
picar to nibble at, pick at
pie, el foot
pierna, la leg
pijamas, los pajamas
píldora, la pill
piloto, el pilot
pimienta, la pepper
pintura, la painting
piñata, la colorful suspended container made of papier maché

piscina, la pool
pista, la runway
placer, el pleasure
plano, el map (of a city)
plata, la silver
plátano, el banana
plato, el plate, dish
plato internacional, el foreign dish
plato principal, el main dish
playa, la beach
plaza, la town square
pobre poor
poco little
poco a poco little by little
poder (ue) to be able, can
pollo, el chicken
poncho, el poncho, blanket used over shoulders
poner to put
poner la tele to put on the T.V.
popular popular
por for, through
por allá over there
por aquí around here
por avión by plane
por ciento percent
por ejemplo for example
por eso therefore
por favor please
por lo menos at least
¿por qué? why
porque because
postre, el dessert
por supuesto of course
practicar to practice
precio, el price
preferir (ie) to prefer
pregunta, la question
preguntar to ask (a question)
premio, el prize
preparar to prepare

presentación, la
introduction, presentation
presentar   to present,
introduce
préstamo, el   loan
prestar   to lend
primavera, la   spring
primero   first
primo/a el, la   cousin
prisa, la   haste
probar (ue)   to taste, try, try
on
problema, el   problem
profesión, la   profession
profesor, el   teacher, professor
(m)
profesora, la   teacher,
professor (f)
programador de
computadoras, el   computer
programmer (m)
programadora de
computadoras, la   computer
programmer (f)
prohibido   forbidden,
prohibited
propina, la   tip
psicóloga, la   psychologist (f)
psicólogo, el   psychologist (m)
pueblo, el   small town
puerta, la   door
puerto, el   port
pues   then, well then
puesto de gasolina, el
gasoline pump station
puesto que   since
pulóver, el   sweater
pulsera, la   bracelet
purpúreo   purple

Q

que   than
¡qué....!   What a .....!
¿que?   what ?
¡Qué lástima!   What a shame!
¡Qué pena!   What a pity! How
sad!
¿Que tal?   How's it going?
quedarse   to stay, remain
querer (ie)   to like, love, want
querido   dear
queso, el   cheese
¿quién?   who, whom
quisiera   I would like

R

radio, el   radio set
radio, la   radio
rápido   rapid, quickly
rascacielos, el   skyscraper
ratón, el   mouse
razón, la   reason
rebajar   to lower, to mark
down
receta, la   recipe, prescription
recibir   to receive
recién   recently
refrescos, los   refreshments
refrigerador, el   refrigerator
regalo, el   gift
regatear   to bargain
relámpago, el   flash of
lightening
reloj de pulsera, el   wrist
watch
repetir (i)   to repeat
Repita usted.   Repeat.
reservación, la   reservation
reservar   to reserve
respirar   to breathe
restaurante, el   restaurant

retirar   to withdraw
reunión, la   meeting, gathering
revista, la   magazine
rico   rich
riesgo, el   risk
roc, el   rock music
rojo   red
rollo, el   roll (of film)
ron, el   rum
ropa, la   clothing
ropa, interior, la   underwear
rosado   pink
rosbif, el   roast beef
rubio   blond
ruido, el   noise

S
sábana, la   sheet
saber   to know, to know how to
sabor, el   taste, flavor
sacar fotos   to take snapshots
sal, la   salt
sala, la   living room
sala de espera, la   waiting room
salida, la   exit
salir   to leave, go out
salud, la   health
!Salud!   Good health! Here's to you!
saludar   to greet
saludo, el   greeting
salvar   to save (a life)
sandwich, el   sandwich
sangría, la   drink made with red wine and fruit
sano   healthy
seco   dry
secretario/a el, la   secretary
sed, la   thirst
según   according to

segundo   second
seguro, el   insurance
seguro de vida, el   life insurance
sello, el   stamp
semana, la   week
pecho, el   bosom, bust
señor, el   gentleman, Mr.
señora, la   woman, Mrs.
señorita, la   young woman, Miss
sentarse (ie)   to sit down, be seated
sentir (ie)   to feel, to feel sorry
ser   to be
ser humano, el   human being
servicio, el   service
servicios, los   toilets
servir (i)   to serve
si   if, whether
sí   yes
SIDA, el   AIDS
¡Si Dios quiere!   God willing!
siempre   always
siesta, la   nap
siguiente   following
silla, la   chair
sillón, el   armchair
simpático   nice
sin   without
sin duda   doubtless, no doubt
sin embargo   nevertheless
sino   but, but rather
síntoma, el   symptom
sinvergüenza, el, la   rascal, scoundrel
sírvase   please
sobre   on, over
sobre, el   envelope
sobrina, la   niece
sobrino, el   nephew
¡Socorro!   Help!

sofá, el   sofa
sol, el   sun
soldado, el   soldier
solicitar un empleo   to apply for a job
soltero   single
sombrero, el   hat
sopa, la   soup
sorprendido   surprised
sostén, el   brassiere
sótano, el   basement
subir   to go up, board
sucio   dirty
suegra, la   mother-in-law
suegro, el   father-in-law
sueldo, el   salary
sueño, el   sleepiness, dream
suerte, la   luck
suéter, el   sweater
sufrir   to suffer
suma, la   amount
supermercado, el   supermarket

T

taberna, la   bar
tal   such
tal vez   perhaps, maybe
tamaño, el   size
también   also, too
tampoco   neither, not either
tampón, el   tampon
tan   as
tantos   as many
tapa, la   hors d'oeuvre taken at a bar
tarde   late
tarde, la   afternoon
tarjeta de crédito, la   credit card
tarjeta postal, la   post card
taxi, el   taxi

taza, la   cup
té, el   tea
teatro, el   theater
tele, la   T.V.
teléfono, el   telephone
telenovela, la   soap opera
televisión, la   television
temprano   early
tenedor, el   fork
tener   to have
tener éxito   to be lucky
tener que   to have to
teñir   to tint, color
tenis, el   tennis
termómetro, el   thermometer
tertulia, la   informal social gathering
testigo, el   witness
ti   you
tía, la   aunt
tiempo, el   weather, time
tienda, la   store
tienda de comestibles, la   grocery store
tío, el   uncle
tíos, los   uncles, uncles and aunts
típico   typical
tipo de cambio, el   exchange rate
toalla, la   towel
toallas higiénicas, las   sanitary pads
tocar   to touch, play (a musical instrument)
tocino, el   bacon
todo   all, everything
todo el mundo   everybody
todos   everybody
todos los días   every day
tomar   to take, eat, drink
tonto   stupid, foolish

tormenta, la   storm
torta, la   cake
tortilla, la   flat corn pancake, omelet
tos, la   cough
tostador, el   toaster
trabajar   to work
trabajo, el   work, occupation
traducir   to translate
traer   to bring
traje, el   suit
traje de bano, el   bathing suit
trascocina, la   utility room
tratar de   to try to
tren, el   train
triste   sad
trueno, el   thunder
tu   your (fam.)

U

¡Uf!   Phew! Ugh!
un momento   a moment, just a minute
un poco   a little
universidad, la   university
usar   to use
útil   useful
uva, la   grape

V

vacaciones, las   vacation
valer   to be worth
varios   several
vaso, el   glass
vecino/a, el, la   neighbor
vender   to sell
venir   to come
ventana, la   window
ver   to see
verano, el   summer
verdad, la   truth

verde   green
verduras, las   greens
vergüenza, la   shame
vez, la   time, occasion
vía, la   track
viajar   to travel
viaje, el   trip
viaje de negocios, el   business trip
vida, la   life
videocasette, el   video tape
viejo   old
viento, el   wind
vino, el   wine
vino blanco, el   white wine
vino rojo, el   red wine
visa, la   visa
visita, la   visit
visitar   to visit
vista, la   sight, vision
visto   seen
viuda, la   widow
viudo, el   widower
vivir   to live
volar (ue)   to fly
volver (ue)   to return
vómitos, los   vomiting
vuelo, el   flight
vuelto   returned

Y

y   and
ya   already
yerno, el   son-in-law
yodo, el   iodine
Yo no.   Not me.

Z

zapatilla, la   slipper
zapato, el   shoe

A

according to   según
a few   algunos
a lot of   mucho
ability   la habilidad
abortion   el aborto
abroad   al extranjero
accident   el accidente
accompany   acompañar
activity   la actividad
actor   el actor
actress   la actriz
address   la dirección
adhesive tape   el esparadrapo
advertisement   el anuncio
affectionate   cariñoso
after   después de
afternoon   la tarde
afterwards   después
again   de nuevo, otra vez
against   contra
aha!   ¡ajá!
ahead   adelante
AIDS   el SIDA
air conditioned   aire acondicionado
air mail   el correo aéreo
airline   la línea aérea
airplane   el avión
airport   el aeropuerto
all   todo
allergic   alérgico
almost   casi
already   ya
also   también
always   siempre
among   entre

amount   la suma
amusement   el divertimiento, la diversión
and   y
angry   enfadado
anniversary   el aniversario
annoy   molestar
another   otro
answer   contestar
any   alguno
any at all   cualquier
anything   algo
apartment   el apartmento
apartment house   el edificio de apartamentos
apparently   al parecer
appendix   el apéndice
appetite   el apetito
apple   la manzana
apply for a job   solicitar un empleo
as   tan
as, like   como
as many   tantos
as much   tanto
appointment   la cita
architect   el arquitecto, la arquitecta
arm   el brazo
armchair   el sillón
around here   por aquí
arrival   la llegada
arrive   llegar
article   el artículo
artist   el/la artista
ask (for something)   pedir (i)

ask (a question) preguntar
aspirin la aspirina
assure asegurar
astronaut el/la astronauta
at a
at first al principio
at home en casa
at least por lo menos
at midnight a medianoche
at noon a mediodía
at the same time a la vez
atmosphere el ambiente
aunt la tía
automobile el automóvil
autumn el otoño

B

back el dorso
backward atrás
bacon el tocino
bad malo
badly mal
bakery shop la panadería
ball point pen el bolígrafo
banana el plátano
bank el banco
bar la taberna
barber el barbero
barber shop la peluquería
bargain la ganga
bargain regatear
baseball el béisbol
basement el sótano
bath el baño
bathing suit el traje de baño
bathroom el baño
be estar, ser
be able to poder (ue)
be in a good mood estar de buen humor
be in love with estar enamorado de

be named llamarse
be on a diet estar a dieta
be on vacation estar de vacaciones
be quiet callarse
be lucky tener suerte
be successful tener éxito
beach la playa
bean el frijol
beautiful hermoso
because porque
become angry enojarse
bed la cama
bedroom el dormitorio
beef la carne de res
beer la cerveza
before antes de
begin empezar (ie)
behind atrás, detrás de
believe creer
beside al lado de
besides además
better mejor
between entre
bill la cuenta
bird el pájaro
birthday el cumpleaños
black negro
black coffee el café negro
blond rubio
blue azul
board (a vehicle) subir
body el cuerpo
book el libro
borrow pedir (i) prestado
boss el jefe (m)
boss la jefa (f)
bosom, bust el pecho
both ambos, los dos
bottle la botella
box la caja
boy (little) el niño
boyfriend el novio

bracelet   la pulsera
brassiere   el sostén
Bravo!   ¡Olé!
bread   el pan
breakfast   el desayuno
breathe   respirar
bridge (card game)   el bridge-contrato
bring   traer
brother   el hermano
brother-in-law   el cuñado
brother, little   hermanito
brothers, brothers and sisters   los hermanos
brown   moreno
building   el edificio
bullfight   la corrida de toros
bus   el autobús
business   los negocios
business man   el hombre de negocios
business trip   el viaje de negocios
busy   ocupado
but   pero
but rather   sino
butcher's shop   la carnicería
butter   la mantequilla
buttocks   las nalgas
buy   comprar
by the way   a propósito
by plane   por avión

C

cake   la torta
calculator   la calculadora
calendar   el calendario
Calm down!   ¡Cálmate!
calorie   la caloría
camera   la cámara
camp   acampar
can   la lata

can   poder (ue)
captain   el capitán
car   el carro, el coche
care   el cuidado
carpenter   el carpintero
carry   llevar
cash a check   cambiar (cobrar) un cheque
cat   el gato
cathedral   el catedral
cent   el centavo
center   el centro
certain   cierto
chair   la silla
champagne   el champaña
change   cambiar
change, small change   el cambio
channel   el canal
chat   charlar
cheap   barato
check   el cheque
checkbook   la chequera
cheese   el queso
chest   el pecho
chicken   el pollo
children   los hijos
chocolate   el chocolate
church   la iglesia
city   la ciudad
class   la clase
clean   limpiar
clean   limpio
clerk   el/la dependiente/a
client   el/la cliente
climate   el clima
close   cerrar (ie)
closet   el armario
clothing   la ropa
club   el club
coast   la costa
coat   el abrigo
cockroach   la cucaracha

cocktail   el coctel
coffee   el café
cold   frío
color   el color
color   teñir
comb one's hair   peinarse
come   venir
Come in.   Pase Ud.
comfortable   cómodo
company   la compañía
computer programmer   el programador, la programadora de computadoras
concern   el cuidado
condom   el condón
confirm   confirmar
Congratulations!   ¡Felicitaciones!
contented   contento
converse   conversar
cook   cocinar
cook   el cocinero
cookie   el bizcocho
cool   fresco
cornflakes   los cornflés
correct   correcto
cost   costar (ue)
costume   el disfraz
cough   la tos
counter   el mostrador
country   el país
countryside   el campo
courtyard   el patio
cousin   el/la primo/a
cramps   los calambres
crazy   loco
cream   la crema
credit card   la tarjeta de crédito
cruel   cruel
cup   la taza
currency   la moneda
custard (carmelized)   el flan

customer   el/la cliente
customs   la aduana
cut   cortar

D

dance   bailar
dance   el baile
dangerous   peligroso
dark   moreno
date (appointment)   la cita
date   la fecha
daughter   la hija
daughter-in-law   la nuera
day   el día
dead   muerto
dear   caro, querido
declare   declarar
delicious   delicioso
Delighted.   Encantado.
dentist   el/la dentista
depart   partir
department store   el almacén
deposit   depositar
dessert   el postre
deserve   merecer
desire   desear
diabetes   la diabetes
dial the number   marcar el número
diarrhea   la diarrea
die   morir (ue)
diet   la dieta
difficult   difícil
diligent   diligente
dining room   el comedor
diplomat   el/la diplomático/a
dirty   sucio
disco   la discoteca
discotheque   la discoteca
dish   el plato
divorced   divorciado
do   hacer

doctor   el médico
dog   el perro
doll   la muñeca
dollar   el dólar
done   hecho
door   la puerta
doubtless   sin duda
downtown   el centro
dream   el sueño
drink   beber, tomar
drink (carbonated)   la gaseosa
drive   conducir, manejar
driver's license   el carnet de conducir
drugstore   la droguería
dry   seco
drunk   borracho
during   durante

E

each   cada
early   temprano
earn   ganar
earring   el arete
easy   fácil
eat   comer, tomar
efficient   eficiente
egg   el huevo
embrace   abrazar
emergency   la emergencia
employee   empleado/a el, la
enclosed   incluido
engineer   el ingeniero
entertain   entretener
entertaining   divertido
entertainment   el divertimiento, la diversión
entrance   la entrada
entry   la entrada
envelope   el sobre
estimate   estimar
evening meal   la cena

every   cada
everybody   todo el mundo, todos
every day   todos los días
everything   todo
excellent   excelente
exchange rate   el tipo de cambio
excuse me   perdón
exercise   el ejercicio
exit   la salida
expensive   caro
eye   el ojo

F

face   la cara
failure   el fracaso
family   la familia
famous   famoso
fantastic   fantástico
far   lejos
fasten the seat belt   abrochar el cinturón
fat   gordo
father   el padre
father-in-law   el suegro
favor   el favor
favorite   favorito
fear   el miedo
feel   sentir (ie)
feel sorry   sentir (ie)
fever   la fiebre
field   el campo
fill out   llenar
film (movie)   la película
finger   el dedo
fire   despedir (i)
fireworks   los fuegos artificiales
first   primero
first class ticket   el boleto de primera clase

fish el pescado
flight el vuelo
flight attendant el aeromozo, la azafata
fly ir en avión, volar (ue)
food los comestibles, la comida
foolish tonto
following siguiente
foot el pie
for para, por
for example por ejemplo
forbidden prohibido
foreign extranjero
foreign dish el plato internacional
forest el bosque
forever para siempre
fork el tenedor
forward adelante
fourth part el cuarto
free drink la bebida gratuita
French fried potatoes las papas fritas
fresh fresco
friend el amigo, la amiga
fritter el churro
from desde, de
from time to time de vez en cuando
fruit las frutas
full lleno
furniture los muebles

G

game el juego
garage el garaje
garden el jardín
gas pump station el puesto de gasolina
gas service station la estación de gasolina
gathering la reunión

gauge estimar
gentleman el señor
get fat engordar
get married casarse
get up levantarse
gift el regalo
girl (little) la niña
girlfriend la novia
give dar
glass el vaso
glass of champagne la copa de champaña
glasses los anteojos
glove el guante
go ir
go by plane ir en avión
go shopping ir de compras
go up subir
go to bed acostarse (ue)
God Dios
God willing si Dios quiere
gold el oro
good bueno
Good appetite! ¡Buen provecho!
good-bye adiós
Good Health! ¡Salud!
good-looking guapo
gosh! ¡caramba!
grandaughter la nieta
grandfather el abuelo
grandma la abuelita
grandmother la abuela
grandparents los abuelos
grandson el nieto
grape la uva
gray gris
great estupendo
green verde
greens las verduras
greet saludar
greeting el saludo
groceries los comestibles

grocery store   la tienda de comestibles
guitar   la guitarra
guy   el chico

H

hair   el pelo
hairdresser   el/la peluquero/a
hairdresser's shop   la peluquería
half   medio
ham   el jamón
hamburger   la hamburguesa
hand   la mano
hand over   entregar
handbag   el bolso
handkerchief   el pañuelo
handsome   guapo
happen   pasar
happy   contento, feliz
hard liquor   el aguardiente
haste   la prisa
hat   el sombrero
have   tener
Have a good trip!   ¡Buen viaje!
have a good time   divertirse (ie)
have a party   hacer una fiesta
have to   tener que
have just   acabar de
head   la cabeza
health   la salud
healthy   sano
hear   oír
heart   el corazón
heat   el calor
heavy   pesado
Hello! (telephone)   ¡Bueno!, ¡Diga!, ¡Aló!
hello   hola

help   ayudar
Help!   ¡Socorro!
here   aquí
high   alto
highway   la autopista, la carretera
hobby   la diversión, el pasatiempo
holiday   el día de fiesta, la fiesta
home   la casa
home (after a verb of motion)   a casa
honeymoon   la luna de miel
hope   esperar
hors d'oeuvres   las tapas
hospital   el hospital
hot (highly seasoned)   picante
hot dog   el perro caliente
hotel   el hotel
hour   la hora
house   la casa
housewife   el ama (f) de casa
how   ¿cómo?
how many   ¿cuántos/ as?
how much   ¿cuánto?
How's it going?   ¿Qué tal?
hug   el abrazo
hug   abrazar
human   humano
human being   el ser humano
hunger   el hambre (f)
hurt   doler (ue)
husband   el esposo

I

I believe so.   Creo que sí.
I'm glad.   Me alegro.
ice   el hielo
ice cream   el helado
if   si
illness   la enfermedad

important   importante
in   en
in front of   delante de
in order to   para
in the open air   al aire libre
included   incluido
income   los ingresos
inexpensive   barato
injection   la inyección
injury   la herida
insomnia   el insomnio
instead of   en vez de
intend (to)   pensar(ie) en
interest   el interés
interesting   interesante
international   internacional
introduction   la presentación
introduce   presentar
invitation   la invitación
invite   invitar
iodine   el yodo
It depends.   Depende.
it is necessary to   hay que
it is raining   llueve
it is snowing   nieva
I would like   Quisiera

J

jacket   la chaqueta
jam   la confitura
jealous   celoso
jewelry   las joyas
job   el empleo
journalist   el periodista
just a minute   un momento

K

kiss   besar
kiss   el beso
kitchen   la cocina

kitchen utensils   la batería de cocina
knife   el cuchillo
know (a fact, how to do something) saber
know (be aquainted with) conocer

L

lady   la dama
large   grande
last   durar
last night   anoche
late   tarde
late afternoon snack   la merienda
later   después, más tarde
laundry   la lavandería
lawyer   el abogado, la abogada
learn   aprender
leather   el cuero
leave (go out)   salir
left side   la izquierda
leg   la pierna
lemonade   la limonada
lend   prestar
less   menos
lesson   la lección
Let's hope so!   ¡Ojalá!
Let's see.   A ver.
letter   la carta
library   la biblioteca
life   la vida
life insurance   el seguro de vida
lightening (flash of)   el relámpago
like   querer, gustar
likewise   igualmente
listen (to)   escuchar
little   pequeño
little bit   poco

little by little   poco a poco
live   vivir
living room   la sala
loan   el préstamo
long   largo
look (at)   mirar
look (for)   buscar
lose   perder (ie)
lose weight   perder (ie) peso
love   el amor
love   querer
lovely   hermoso
lower (the price)   rebajar
luck   la suerte
luggage   el equipaje
lunch   el almuerzo
luxurious   lujoso

M

mad   loco
made   hecho
magazine   la revista
mail   el correo
mail a letter   echar una carta
al buzón
mailbox   el buzón
mailman   el cartero
main dish   el plato principal
make   hacer
make-up   el maquillaje
man   el hombre
manager   el jefe, la jefa
manner   la manera
many   muchos
map   el mapa
marital   matrimonial
market   el mercado
married   casado
married couple   el
matrimonio
marvelous   maravilloso

mask   la máscara
maybe   tal vez
me   mí
meal   la comida
meat   la carne
mechanic   el mecánico
medicine   la medicina
meet (for the first time)
conocer
meeting   la reunión
menu   el menú
midnight   la medianoche
milk   la leche
mineral water   el agua (f)
mineral
minute   el minuto
mirror   el espejo
miscarriage   el aborto
modern   moderno
moment   el momento
money   el dinero
money order   el giro postal
month   el mes
more   más
more than ever   más que
nunca
morning   la mañana
mother   la madre
mother-in-law   la suegra
motor   el motor
mouse   el ratón
mouth   la boca
movie theater   el cine
movies   el cine
much   mucho
muscle   el músculo
music   la música
must   deber
My pleasure.   El gusto es mío.
My goodness!   ¡Dios mío!
my   mi, mis

N

name   el nombre
nap   la siesta
nationality   la nacionalidad
near   al lado de, cerca de
necessary   necesario
necklace   el collar
need   necesitar
neighbor   el/la vecino/a
neither   ni
neither.....nor   ni.....ni
nephew   el sobrino
never   nunca
nevertheless   sin embargo
new   nuevo
news   las noticias
newspaper   el periódico
next   luego
nibble   picar
nice   simpático
niece   la sobrina
night   la noche
no   no
noise   el ruido
none   ninguno
nobody   nadie
noon   el mediodía
no-one   nadie
nor   ni
nose   la nariz
Not me!   ¡Yo no!
nothing   nada
nowadays   hoy en día
number   el número
nurse   el/ la emfermero/a
nut   la nuez

O

occupation   el oficio, el trabajo
of   de
of course   claro, por supuesto

office   la oficina
often   a menudo
oh!   ¡ay!
Oh, my!   ¡Ay de mi!
oil   el aceite
okay   bueno
old   viejo
omelet   tortilla
on   sobre, en
on board   a bordo de
on foot (walking)   a pie
only   no más
on the contrary   al contrario
one must   hay que
onion   la cebolla
open   abierto
open   abrir
open air   el aire libre
open an account   abrir una cuenta
opened   abierto
or   o
orange (color)   anaranjado
orange (fruit)   la naranja
orange juice   el jugo de naranjas
orchestra   la orquesta
other   otro
ought to   deber
our   nuestro
outdoors   el aire libre
over there   por allá
owner   el dueño

P

pack one's suitcase   hacer la maleta
package   el paquete
pain   doler (ue)
painting   la pintura
pajamas   los pijamas
palace   el palacio

pancake la tortilla
pants los pantalones
paper el papel
paper money el billete de banco
parade el desfile
parcel post package el paquete postal
Pardon me (I didn't hear you) ¿Dígame?
parents los padres
park aparcar
part la parte
party la fiesta
passenger el pasajero
passport el pasaporte
pastime el pasatiempo
pastry el pastel
pay pagar
pea el guisante
pencil el lápiz
penicillin la penicilina
people la gente
pepper la pimienta
per cent por ciento
perfume shop la perfumería
perhaps tal vez
permission el permiso
personal check el cheque personal
pharmacy la farmacia
Phew! ¡Uf!
piano el piano
pick at picar
picked cogido
picture el cuadro
pill la píldora
pillow la almohada
pilot el piloto
pink rosado
pity la lástima
plate el plato
play (a game) jugar

play (a musical instrument) tocar
play cards jugar a los naipes
play golf jugar al golf
play tennis jugar al tenis
pleasant agradable
please sírvase, por favor
pleasure el gusto, el placer
pocket el bolsillo
polite cortés
pool la piscina
poor pobre
poorly mal
pop corn las palomitas
pop group el conjunto
popular popular
pork la carne de cerdo
port el puerto
porter el mozo
post card la tarjeta postal
post office la casa de correos
postage el franqueo
potato la papa
potato chips las papas fritas
pound la libra
practice practicar
prefer preferir (i)
pregnant embarazada
prepare preparar
prescription la receta
present presentar
presentation la presentación
price el precio
priest el cura
private detective el detective privado
prize el premio
problem el problema
profession el oficio, la profesión
professor el profesor, la profesora
proud orgulloso

psychologist   el/la psicólogo/a
punishment   el castigo
purple   purpúreo
purse   el bolso
put   poner
put on the T.V.   poner la tele
put on weight   engordar

Q

quality   la calidad
quarter   cuarto
question   la pregunta

R

radio   la radio
radio set   el radio
railroad station   la estación de ferrocarril
rain   la lluvia
rain   llover (ue)
raincoat   el impermeable
raining   lloviendo
rascal   el/la sinvergüenza
read   leer
really   de veras
reason   la razón
receive   recibir
recently   recién
recipe   la receta
record   el disco
red   rojo
refreshments   los refrescos
refrigerator   la nevera, el refrigerador
remain   quedarse
relative   el pariente
rent   alquilar
repeat   repetir (i)
Repeat!   ¡Repita Ud.!
request   pedir (i)
reservation   la reserva

rest   descansar
rest   el descanso
restaurant   el restaurante
return (give back)   devolver (ue)
return   volver (ue), regresar
returned   vuelto
rice   el arroz
rich   rico
right (privilege)   el derecho
right side   la derecha
right now   ahora mismo
ring   el anillo
risk   el riesgo
roast beef   el rosbif
rock (music) el roc
roll   el panecillo
roll (of film)   el rollo
room   el cuarto, la cámara, la habitación
roommate   el/la compañero/a de cuarto
rug   la alfombra
rum   el ron
run   correr
runway   la pista

S

sad   triste
said   dicho
Saint's day   el día de santo
salad   ensalada
salary   el sueldo
salt   la sal
sandwich   el sandwich
sanitary pads   las toallas higiénicas
sausage (pork)   el chorizo
save (money)   ahorrar
save (a life)   salvar
say   decir
say goodbye   despedirse (i) de

scale la balanza	**ski** esquiar
school la escuela	**skill** la habilidad
scoundrel el/la sinvergüenza	**skinny** flaco
season la estación	**skirt** la falda
seat el asiento	**sky** el cielo
seat belt el cinturón de seguridad	**skyscraper** el rascacielos
second segundo	**sleep** dormir (ue)
secretary el/la secretario/a	**sleepiness** el sueño
see ver	**slender** delgado
seen visto	**slim down** adelgazar
see you soon hasta luego	**slipper** la zapatilla
see you tomorrow hasta mañana	**slowly** despacio
sell vender	**small** pequeño
send mandar	**smoke** fumar
servant el mozo (m), la moza (f)	**snack** el bocadillo
serve servir (i)	**snow** nevar (ie)
service el servicio	**snowing** nevando
set hair marcar el pelo	**so** tan
several varios	**soap** el jabón
sew coser	**soap opera** la telenovela
shame la vergüenza	**social gathering** (informal) la tertulia
shave afeitarse	**socks** los calcetines
sheet la sábana	**sofa** el sofá
shirt la camisa	**soldier** el soldado
shoe el zapato	**some** alguno, algunos
shop assistant el/la dependiente/a	**somebody** alguien
shout gritar	**someone** alguien
sick enfermo	**something** algo
sickness la enfermedad	**son** el hijo
side el lado	**son-in-law** el yerno
sight la vista	**song** la canción
sign el letrero	**so, so** (all right) así, así
sign firmar	**soup** la sopa
silver la plata	**speak** hablar
since puesto que	**spend** gastar
single soltero	**spend time** pasar
sister la hermana	**spoiled** mimado
sister-in-law la cuñada	**spoon** la cuchara
sit sentarse (ie)	**sport** el deporte
size el tamaño	**spring** la primavera
	stamp el sello
	stand in line hacer cola

stand up   levantarse
state   el estado
station   la estación
stay   quedarse
steak   el bistec
stockings   las medias
stomach   el estómago
store   la tienda
storm   la tormenta
stove   la estufa
street   la calle
student   el, la estudiante
study   estudiar
stupid   tonto
subway   el metro
such   tal
suffer   sufrir
sugar   el azúcar
suit   el traje
suitcase   la maleta
summer   el verano
sun   el sol
sunstroke   la insolación
supermarket   el supermercado
sure   cierto
surprised   sorprendido
sweater   el pulóver, el suéter
sweet   dulce
swim   nadar
symptom   el síntoma

T

table   la mesa
take   tomar
take a trip   hacer un viaje
take a bath   bañarse
take one's leave   despedirse (i) de
take snapshots   sacar fotos
talk   hablar
tall   alto

tampon   el tampón
tape   la cinta
taste   el gusto
taste   probar (ue)
taxi   el taxi
tea   el té
teach   enseñar
teacher   el professor, la profesora
team   el equipo
teaspoon   la cucharita
telephone   el teléfono
telephone number   el número de teléfono
television   la televisión
tell   decir
tennis   el tenis
than   que
thank Heaven!   ¡gracias a Dios!
thank you   gracias
that   ese, esa
That will do!   ¡Basta!
That's all.   Eso es todo.
That's right!   ¡Eso es!
theater   el teatro
the same to you   igualmente
then   entonces, luego
there   allá
there is, there are   hay
thermometer   el termómetro
these   estos, estas
thin   flaco
think   pensar (ie)
thing   la cosa
thirst   la sed
this   este, esta
those   esos, esas
through   por
thunder   el trueno
ticket   el boleto
ticket, bill (paper money) el billete

tie   la corbata
time   la hora
time (occasion)   la vez
tint   teñir
tired   cansado
to   a
to be pleasing to, to like   gustar
to be worth   valer
toast   el pan tostado
toaster   el tostador
today   hoy
toilet paper   el papel higiénico
toilets   los servicios
tomorrow   mañana
too   también
too much   demasiado
tooth   el diente
toothbrush   el cepillo de dientes
tooth paste   la pasta dentrífica
touch   tocar
tourist class ticket   el boleto de turista
tourist guide booklet   la guía turística
toward   hacia
towel   la toalla
town   el pueblo
town square   la plaza
toy   el juguete
track   la vía
train   el tren
translate   traducir
travel   viajar
travel agency   la agencia de viajes
traveler's check   el cheque de viaje
trip   el viaje
trousers   los pantalones
truth   la verdad
try, try on   probar (ue)

try (to)   tratar de
T.V.   la tele
two way ticket   el billete de ida y vuelta
typical   típico

U

Ugh!   ¡Uf!
ugly   feo
umbrella   el paraguas
uncle   el tío
uncle(s) and aunt(s)   los tíos
under   debajo de
understand   entender (ie)
underwear   la ropa interior
unfortunately   desgraciadamente
university   la universidad
until   hasta
use   usar
useful   útil
usual, usually   de costumbre
utility room   la trascocina

V

vacation   las vacaciones
VCR   el magnetoscopio
vegetable   la legumbre
vegetable garden   el huerto
very   muy
video tape   el videocasette
visa   la visa
vision   la vista
visit   la visita
visit   visitar
vomiting   los vómitos

W

wait   esperar

waiter   el camarero, el mozo
waiting room   la sala de espera
waitress   la camarera, la moza
walk   caminar
wallet   la cartera
want   desear, querer
wash   lavar
wash oneself   lavarse
washing machine   la lavadora
Watch out!   ¡Cuidado!
water   el agua (f)
way   la manera
weak   débil
wear   llevar
wedding   la boda
week   la semana
weekend   el fin de semana
weigh   pesar
Welcome!   ¡Bienvenido!
well   bien
well then   pues
wet   mojado
weather   el tiempo
what   que
What a shame!   ¡Qué lástima! ¡Qué pena!
when   cuando
when?   ¿cuándo?
where? (motion involved)   ¿adónde?
where?   ¿dónde?
whether   si
which? (one)   ¿cuál?
white   blanco
who, whom?   ¿quién?
why?   ¿por qué?
wide   ancho
widow   la viuda
widower   el viudo
wife   la esposa

win   ganar
wind   el viento
window   la ventana
wine   el vino
wine, red   el vino rojo
wine, white   el vino blanco
winter   el invierno
with   con
withdraw   retirar
with me   conmigo
without   sin
with you (fam)   contigo
witness   el testigo
woman   la mujer, la señora
wonderful   estupendo
woods   el bosque
work   trabajar
work   el trabajo
workday   el día de trabajo
would you (form) like?   ¿le gustaría?
wound   la herida
wrist watch   el reloj (de pulsera)
write   escribir
written   escrito

Y

year   el año
yellow   amarillo
yes   sí
yesterday   ayer
you (fam)   ti
your (fam)   tu
You don't say!   ¡No me digas!
young   joven
young boy   el chico
young girl   la chica
young woman   la señorita

Z

"Zip" code   el distrito postal

124